Simon Gray: Fou

Simon Gray was born in 1936 in Hayling Island.
He lives in London with his wife, two cats and a dog.

SIMON GRAY

Four Plays

The Pig Trade
Japes Too
Michael
The Holy Terror

Introduced by the author

ff

faber and faber

This collection first published in 2004
by Faber and Faber Limited
3 Queen Square London WC1N 3AU
Published in the United States by Faber and Faber Inc.
an affiliate of Farrar, Straus and Giroux LLC, New York

Typeset by Country Setting, Kingsdown, Kent CT14 8ES
Printed in England by Mackays of Chatham plc, Chatham, Kent

A CIP record for this book
is available from the British Library

0-571-21988-8

2 4 6 8 10 9 7 5 3 1

For Judy

Contents

Introduction

I've just come across an interview given by a fellow playwright in which he describes one of his plays as the first of his maturity. How did he know? is what I want to know; how could he tell? Because while I can see that there's quite a lot about me that is actually quite old, I can't find anything to suggest that I'm mature, at least mature enough to have produced the works of my maturity, though of course it may be that I've produced them but am not yet mature enough to identify them. The odds are, though, that I'm not subject to any kind of evolution, particularly conscious evolution. For one thing, I've always believed – or think I have – that the hereness-and-nowness of life is virtually all there is of it, which of course explains why it is so difficult to grasp and get down in the hereness-and-nowness of writing, but doesn't explain why ninety per cent of my writing life seems to be spent in rewriting, and why it's so hard to find the whatever it is – perhaps a burst of imagination? – that will spring me from the drudgery of recycling yet another draft of dead here-and-now, into the exhilarating here-and-now of not knowing what the next sentence will be even as I write it – though feeling pretty sure that it will be the right one, must be the right one, since the next sentence is following almost simultaneously. Of course this doesn't mean that I will end up with a good play, only that I will have written a whole version of the play that I can no longer remember starting out to write, and that when I have written the last words of its last scene I can stop at last – though one of the troubles with the here-and-now is that it lacks punctuation, especially full stops – and sometimes, long after the play has been staged,

I find myself back at its beginning, about to write its first words again.

I finished the first version of *The Holy Terror* in the late summer of 1986. It was called *Melon* and like its successor was about a high-flying publisher who advocates promiscuity for his wife and himself, then has a nervous breakdown when he decides, against all available evidence, that his wife is having an affair with one of his best friends – which best friend being the conundrum that finally drives him mad. It was produced the following spring at the Theatre Royal, Haymarket, and played to good houses, thanks mainly to Alan Bates, whose performance as the brute Englishman with a chaotic soul was so dazzling that I suspected it flattered the text – anyway, there was a discrepancy between the story that the play told and the story that Alan told that made me feel, every time I sat through the production, that the play didn't quite work. Of course I also told myself that it was too late to think about it, let alone fret about it, move on, move on, and I did eventually move on, writing another stage play and some television plays, until one day, long after *Melon* had closed, I found myself thinking about it again, then fretting about it again, then sitting down to write it again, and finally, after drafts and drafts and more drafts, I was in possession of a new play that was like the old play in its story and its characters, but so different in its narrative form that I felt that it required a title of its own. *The Holy Terror* was first performed in October 1989 on BBC Radio Three in a fine production directed by Jane Morgan, with James Laurenson as Melon. In February 1991 I directed it myself, at the Temple of Arts Theatre in Tucson, Arizona, where it went well enough, but straggled a bit, and needed work. A year later, revised somewhat, it opened at the Promenade Theatre in New York, in a production that you would have described as eccentric if you hadn't known that the director drank quite a bit before each day's rehearsals and quite a bit after them, and more than quite a bit during them, while never losing the conviction, however many times he stumbled down the aisle and tumbled over the seats, often with a lighted cigarette in his mouth and another, also lighted, in the hand that wasn't holding a champagne bottle, that he was in full command of his faculties, and that his genius for cutting through to the centre of things had never burned more fiercely – so, when he had trouble moving the actors around the furniture, he cut the furniture; and thus, when he had trouble deciding between different lighting effects, he cut the lighting. So and thus, on the press night the audience found themselves confronted by unnerved actors performing in house-lights on a mainly empty set, and the actors could see not only the individual faces of the audience, but also the tops of the heads of the critics as they bent over their pads on their knees. The director himself, by the way, frightened, triumphant and drunk, was also highly visible and all over the place, now at the back of the stalls, now at the top of an aisle, now in the dress circle – if I'd been one of the actors I'd have stepped off the stage in the middle of my scene and mur-dered him, right there, under the house-lights, in full view of the critics: the report in the next morning's *New York Times* might at least have marginalised the review. The pro-ducer, who was devoted to the play, made periodic attempts to fire him but was thwarted by his agent, who pointed out that as the director had playwright approval, and as the playwright and the director were one and the same, it would be a question of asking him to fire himself, which he was unlikely to do, as he got on so well together. *The Holy Terror* lay dormant until about a year ago, when it was picked up by a London management. There are plans to produce it in the Spring of 2004, with Simon Callow in the lead.

The first version of the two middle plays in this volume was called *Japes*, and was about two brothers, Michael and Japes, the nature of their love for each other, and for the young woman, Anita, who becomes Michael's wife while remaining Japes's lover. It was first staged at the Mercury Theatre, Colchester, in November 2000, then transferred to the Theatre Royal, Haymarket, in February 2001, with Toby Stephens, Jasper Britton and Claire Swinburne in the three parts, Peter Hall directing. It was a lovely production, I think, and I can't say I was actually dissatisfied with the final form of the play – I cut and rewrote it in rehearsals and in the break between Colchester and London – but every time I sat through it at the Haymarket I felt stirring not so much an improved version as an alternative version: the same characters in the same situation in the same house, but telling a slightly different story through to an almost opposite conclusion. When I sat down to write it, it came out twice, in two different stories, one of which comes to the opposite conclusion, the other to the same conclusion but by an unexpected (at least by me) route. I called the first of the new plays *Japes Too* in order to distinguish it from its predecessor while acknowledging its connection, the other I called *Michael*, for obvious reasons. There is a move to produce *Japes Too* and *Michael* in tandem in New York some time early next year, with Maria Aitken directing.

The Pig Trade is about the turbulent relationship between the art expert Bernard Berenson, and the art dealer, Joseph Duveen. It is set in I Tatti, Berenson's famous villa outside Florence, on a summer's night in 1937, with Mussolini at the height of his power, the Barbarians at the Gates. I started to write it as a screenplay about four years ago, fiddling about with it for months, with diminishing interest and belief, until I abandoned it. My problem was that the heart of the story could only be revealed in the course of an epic confrontation between the two morally crippled Titans, which I couldn't write, perhaps because I knew in my bones that however I approached it, and against my every decent inclination, it would come out stagey. The solution, as a friend pointed out, was to write it for the stage, which I did. The first scenes, establishing Berenson and his household, his wife Mary, his mistress Nicky and Duveen's emissary Fowles, came easily enough – in fact I spent a great deal of unnecessary time in their company, in scenes that don't appear in the final play, simply because I enjoyed them so much, and because they delayed the moment when I'd have to get down to my dramatic muttons, with the entrance of Duveen. This comes just after Berenson has had a rather complicated domestic evening, full of love, anger, apprehension and sex, and is now alone in his study, making peace with himself, ready for a final, restful spot of work. He adjusts his lamp, picks up a folder, the door bursts open, the detested Duveen enters, Berenson looks at him aghast, Duveen opens his arms to embrace him – I simply couldn't get myself past Duveen frozen with outstretched arms, Berenson frozen aghast. I did the approach again and again, first changing the closing exchanges between Berenson and Nicky, then changing Berenson's actions in his study, finally providing Duveen with offstage footsteps and coughs, hoping that eventually I'd just find myself writing him into the room and the opening lines of the conversation, their last conversation together, the heart of the play. I stopped, waited for a week or so, started, stopped, waited, started, stopped – one night very late, or one morning very early, with my eyes closed, so to speak, I leapt.

Duveen bursts into the room, stretches out his arms. Berenson lets out a laugh of incredulity.

Duveen Happy birthday, BB!

It wasn't Berenson's birthday, actually, but I could sort out why Duveen thought it was, if he did think it was, later, or I could just cut the line or perhaps even decide that it was Berenson's birthday after all – I could do any or all of these things, easy-peasy, now that I'd got them to talk at last – in fact, the problem thereafter was how to get them to stop. *The Pig Trade* is the only one of the four plays in this book not to have been produced on the stage in a previous form – in fact, at the time of writing, not to have been produced at all, although it almost certainly might be, some time between now and then, depending on the availability of actors, theatres, producers, directors, honesty and money.

By way of a postscript: I may never have a mature period, but I've had a drunk period, and am now in a sober period – the first three plays in this volume were written during the latter, the last during the former. This is not a boast, nor a confession, just information which may or may not be interesting to the reader.

P.P.S. The account above of how I directed the New York production of *The Holy Terror* when I was drunk was written by me when sober. My life would be different if it had been the other way around.

P.P.P.S. I've recently started looking at *The Pig Trade* again. I suspect that the version published here may turn out to be merely another draft, under the wrong title.

Simon Gray

THE PIG TRADE

Characters

Nicky

Fowles

BB

Mary

Duveen

Act One

SCENE ONE

The Garden of I Tatti, 1937. A delightful summer evening. There are chairs, a table, a bench – the sense of a much-used area, close to the house. On the table, a tray with glasses, a bottle of white, opened, some letters, documents, of some sort of work in progress. Nicky, an attractive woman in her early fifties, is sitting on the bench, a sun hat pulled elegantly away from her face. She is wearing dark glasses as she peruses a document, suddenly puts it down, stretches almost voluptuously, sits back, closes her eyes, sips wine. Fowles enters. Sees Nicky, stops, looks at her with pleasure.

Nicky (*becomes aware of a presence, opens her eyes slowly, smiles*) Mr Fowles.

Fowles Miss Mariano. (*Comes over, offers his hand.*) I hope I didn't disturb you.

Nicky Not at all. I was just – basking for a moment. Mary said you'd gone for a little nap, did you manage one?

Fowles Actually, I sat at the window, looking out – couldn't resist – one of my favourite views, you know, looking across to the chapel in the garden, and in that light!

Nicky Ah, the light – yes, BB was just saying that you have a feeling for our landscape.

Fowles (*laughs*) Was he now? He usually accuses me of trying to imagine it into a golf course.

Nicky I'm to tell you he's in the library.

Fowles Ah. And how is he?

Nicky You'll have to be at your most diplomatic. That's how he is.

Fowles Oh dear. Diplomacy's not really my – my –

Nicky Yes it is. That's why Joe sends you – you're one of nature's diplomats, you see, everything you say seems true and honest simply because it comes from you.

Fowles Well, I hope it's because what I say is true and honest – it always is to my knowledge.

Nicky And how is Joe?

Fowles Oh, he's very active, as usual. More active than usual, as a matter of fact.

Nicky Oh dear. Then I'm so glad you're here instead.

Fowles May I have a glass of wine?

Nicky Of course. I would have offered you one before, but I assumed you'd want to go straight to the library.

Fowles No, I don't. I want to talk to you, is what I really mean.

Nicky Is that instead of the glass of wine, or with it?

Fowles Actually, instead. I'm trying not to drink except with meals. If that's all right.

Nicky (*laughing*) It's perfectly all right.

Fowles But I'd love a glass of water.

Nicky (*pours him one*) There.

Fowles May I – may I call you Nicky?

Nicky You usually do at this stage of our conversations.

Fowles Yes, silly, isn't it, how we always start at the beginning? Mr Fowles, Miss Mariano – (*Laughs.*)

Nicky (*smiling*) Well, Edward, now we've dispensed with the niceties, if that's what these are – you have some message from Joe that you want to test out on me first?

Fowles No, no, not a message, but he wants me to ask BB a question, and I'd prefer to know the answer first.

Nicky Why not get it straight from BB?

Fowles If I know the answer I'll ask the question differently, you see.

There is a pause.

Nicky What is it, Mr Fowles – Edward? You seem slightly fraught. I don't believe I've seen you fraught before.

Fowles Yes, well – there was a bit of business on the train. Rather unpleasant. I haven't quite got over it – the police, you see. Well, immigration they said they were, but really I could tell they were the police, looking for spies, I suppose. Took me for a spy – and then they saw his name on one of my papers, Duveen, they said, Joseph Duveen, your employer is Jewish, and Berenson, you are going to visit a Signor Bernard Berenson, also Jewish, possibly? It was all like that, and I kept saying that Mr Duveen was an Anglo-American, I kept stressing American, Joe would have hated that, you know how important being English is to him, especially in America, but now in Italy I've made him into an Anglo-*American* businessman and art lover with a special love of the great Italian artists and that Mr Berenson was the world's greatest expert on the great Italian artists, they both worshipped Italy for her history, her beauty, her people, that's what they were, who they were, neither of them in the slightest sense Jewish in the important sense of the word, etc., etc. – all very shameful, especially when I think of the way I kept referring to the remarkable changes taking place under their *duce* – I think they believed me, well, why shouldn't they, it's true, after all? But what I'm really trying to explain is – is the atmosphere, the arrogance and brutish stupidity – not – not Italian, really. Not my dear old Italy, eh?

There is a pause.

Nicky I know. We feel it too. Especially BB. He jokes about Signor Mussolini, the Duck as he calls him, but really, he is afraid.

Fowles For his life, you mean?

Nicky BB! Afraid for his life! (*Laughs.*) Anyway, they wouldn't dare touch him. He is not some insignificant little Lithuanian Jew, he's an American citizen with an international reputation – 'the living custodian of the Italian inheritance' they call him, in the Duck's – (*Corrects herself with a smile.*) – Signor Mussolini's own newspapers. But he's afraid that a war will sweep this – all of this – all of I Tatti itself and his wonderful collections – into rubble. His dearest wish now is to give it to Harvard University, with which he has always maintained such strong connections. If Harvard accepts, then the future of I Tatti would be guaranteed. But such a gift would almost certainly have to be accompanied by money. Endowments . . . I Tatti is very expensive to keep up, as you know, Edward. At the moment, we are finding it a struggle to keep it going just from day to day. Perhaps you should keep it in mind, Edward, these complicated problems over money, when you go in to speak to BB. It will help you with his temper, perhaps.

Fowles Of course I will, Nicky, I always do – but with respect, with all respect to I Tatti – and I must say I think Harvard would be foolish not to grab it while it can, whatever the cost, – it doesn't constitute the greater part of BB's life's work, does it? His finest achievement, his lasting memorial, is likely to be his writing. Above all, his four masterpieces, his Four Gospels. Without them the world wouldn't be, well, where it is with the Italian painters of the Renaissance, would it? In fact, it wouldn't be anywhere in the Italian Renaissance without them.

Nicky Certainly without them Joe wouldn't be where he is, which is in the market place, selling off the great works of the Italian Renaissance as if they were stocks and shares, their greatness understood because of BB.

Fowles Well, I expect Joe thinks he was pretty well established in the art business before BB turned up with his Four Gospels and all those wonderful Italians. And without Joe in the market place, BB wouldn't be here in I Tatti, would he, trying to create his great memorial to himself for Harvard?

Nicky If it weren't for Joe's money, is that what you're saying? Well, when I said you were a natural diplomat I didn't mean that you were a gunboat.

Fowles What?

Nicky You seem to be issuing threats.

Fowles Threats! Good heavens, Nicky, I'm sorry, I didn't mean – no, no, all I was saying – what was I saying? – oh, yes, I was saying that BB's greatest work isn't this – I Tatti, in all its charms – it's in his books, imperishable.

Nicky Yes, but why are you saying that?

Fowles Why? Well, I don't know, the conversation seemed to be moving in that direction –

Nicky It was dragged there, by you. One moment you were telling me of your experiences with Italian immigration, the next that it didn't matter if I Tatti and its beauty were swept away with the war, because BB had written his Four Gospels, and they were what mattered – have you ever read them, any one of them even, even a chapter in any one of them, by the way, Edward?

Fowles I've looked at all the pictures. And read the captions, miss. Honestly.

Nicky (*laughs*) But of course! Your question! You wanted to remind me that Joe is omnipresent before you asked your question. Well, I am reminded. Now you can ask your question.

Fowles Yes, well, all I really wanted to know is whether there's any truth in the story that Joe has been hearing – that BB has been seeing a certain Roman count.

Nicky (*after a little pause*) There are so many Roman counts, one runs into them all the time, everywhere, but none of them is certain, I assure you, quite a few of them come from Sicily.

Fowles Gianisanti. Il Conte di Gianisanti. Has BB been seeing him?

Nicky You make it sound like a tryst. And why should he not have trysts with this Conte di Gian – (*Gestures.*)

Fowles If he has been advising him about the value of paintings –

Nicky The value? Do you mean the price, Edward? BB advising on the price –

Fowles Attribution. Authenticity. Provenance.

Nicky Ah.

Fowles In other words, value. In other words, price. In other words, it doesn't matter which words one uses, because BB has an exclusive contract with Joe that covers all of them. And if BB's in breach of his contract –

BB (*who has appeared unnoticed, listens to the last few sentences*) What then?

Fowles Well, then Joe wouldn't have to honour his side of the contract, I suppose, BB, is what it would come to.

BB I hope you've had a decent rest. I've been expecting you in the library, where we usually discuss my affairs. (*Going to wine bucket, pours himself a glass of wine.*)

Nicky It's my fault, I waylaid him, BB.

BB sees Fowles's glass, comes over, fills it with wine. Fowles makes to protest, doesn't.

BB (*gently*) You were talking of honour, contracts and so forth, I believe, with my secretary. Should I be sorry I interrupted?

Fowles No, I – well – (*Smiles.*) I expect you heard everything – everything you needed to hear.

BB Yes, weren't you fortunate not to have to say it directly to my face? And then I wouldn't have to say directly to you that a contract has to be honoured on both sides – or not?

Nicky Shall I go and deal with these? (*picking up bills*)

BB (*checks her with a gesture*) Or not?

Fowles In what respect do you think that Joe has failed to honour?

BB Well, only on the money front, perhaps? As his *employee* I note that my wages are on an unusual course –

as the years pass, they diminish. (*to Nicky*) Remind me, my dear girl, what my wages were in 1927?

Nicky In the region of fifty thousand dollars.

BB And these last two years?

Nicky Twenty thousand dollars.

BB From fifty to twenty – and so next year – granted that we're still alive next year, and not in captivity to the Duck, what can we expect next year, if this rate of decline continues? Ten thousand, five thousand – and he complains because I seek for other sources – no, not seek, I don't seek, other sources seek me. After all, who else can they turn to? And what can I do under the circumstances, speaking as a man who is likely to have descended from fifty to five –

Nicky I'm going in.

BB My secretary will answer for me. Tell him what I can do – no, tell him what I did do, with the Conte di Gianisanti?

Nicky Paid him a visit, looked at some paintings, withheld his advice.

Fowles Ah.

BB For the while. I decided to wait for a visit. Either that or a cheque. A cheque – I mean you no discourtesy – would have been preferable. (*Little pause.*) Even when forced into the pig trade, one must try not to behave like the pigs one is trading in. (*Laughs.*) What a completely hopeless metaphor – I would seem to be saying that the great painters of the Renaissance are in fact pigs and that your Joe and I trade in them, whereas of course it is your Joe and I who are the pigs – help me, Nicky, I've tangled myself in a figure of speech.

Fowles Oh, it's all right, I understand you, BB, you're thinking of the pigs in the nursery rhyme, I expect, There's the pig who goes to market, the pig who stays at home, etc., and you're talking of Joe being the one, you the other, but the fact is that the market is the market, and when the market goes into recession and then depression, as it has done, then the market-going pig and the stay-at-home pig both suffer. In other words what I mean is that percentages are percentages, and that's what your contract with Joe deals in, so that when Joe's income drops your percentage remains the same but your income drops too, in proportion as Joe's drops. What's extraordinary, from Joe's point of view, is that while other men were throwing themselves out of windows on Wall Street Joe managed to keep his head above water on Wall Street and keep you on as much as twenty thousand pounds a year, and furthermore there's every reason to believe that if we keep our feet on the ground we may start climbing back to where we were, war or no war, but that would depend on the maintenance of exclusivity, fair's fair, BB.

BB Very well, Edward, I'll accept that, mixed metaphors included – but there is still money outstanding, I believe, is there not, my dear?

Nicky Eighteen and a half thousand pounds.

Fowles I'll ask Joe to settle it as soon as I get back.

BB And?

Fowles And it'll be settled.

Nicky And how couldn't it be, with two such reasonable men? Now I must go and see Mary. (*making to go off*)

BB (*spotting package*) And what is that?

   Nicky comes back.

Something the piggy at the market has sent to the piggy at home, to put a price on? How liberated our speech has become!

Fowles No, no. It's the copy you asked for. I've done it.

BB (*clearly at a loss and uncomfortable*) You've done it?

Fowles Well, I mean, Mme Helfer did it. Just before I left Paris. She asked me to bring it . . . well, have a look, tell me what you think. Of course I couldn't tell the difference, she could have handed me the original – which is on its way to Joe now, by the way. Or perhaps the copy is, eh? (*laughing, either unaware or seemingly unaware of BB's confusion*)

BB (*to Nicky*) My dear, are you still here? Surely Mary is waiting for you.

Nicky So you don't want me to see it, whatever it is?

BB You know what it is. You think I'm hiding it from you?

Takes package from Fowles, rips off the paper, holds it up for her.

There. See. There it is.

Nicky She's done it very well, as usual, Mme Helfer. If it is the copy. (*to Fowles*) Are you sure it is?

BB (*in spite of himself, goes to look*) Yes, she's excelled herself. She's almost a genius, Claudette, but look – here – and here – slightest thinness – almost a signature for almost a genius, but of course, if you think about it, a copier cannot be a genius, it's a contradiction –

Nicky But no one else will know the difference, that's all that matters, isn't it, BB?

BB looks at her, makes to say something angry, gestures helplessly.

Nicky (*to Fowles, going off*) I'll see you at dinner, Mr Fowles.

Fowles Oh, um, well you see –

BB (*cutting in*) I did ask you – I believe I did ask you – to keep this private.

Fowles Well, yes, but I didn't think that included – I'm very sorry, it really didn't occur to me –

BB When I say private I mean, from the women. Otherwise I don't bother to use the word, as I assume that every detail of our business together is kept private from the world.

Fowles I see. Well, it's never come up before. I'll remember it in future, BB, but she seemed to know about it anyway –

BB Yes, yes – it's her feelings, her feelings – Mary's too – well, mine, I admit, mine too. I'm not easy, and they both sense it, and that makes me even less easy.

Fowles But it's for a good cause, isn't it, for some sick men in one of the villages? They'll be getting a bit of money for treatment now, from the priest –

BB Yes.

Fowles Well then.

BB Not men, boys still. Boys sent by the Duck to fight in Abyssinia, poisoned by the Duck's own gas. And I saw the painting in the church entirely by chance, we just happened in one afternoon, I've looked in on all the churches in the area, and one rarely sees anything unexpected, but there, there was this, the original of this, hanging above the altar in a side chapel – I could scarcely believe my eyes, but as my eyes never lie, even in the gloom of a small, unlit church –

Fowles You should see yourself as providence, God's instrument, that kind of thing. What is there to be ashamed of? The church will get money, these lads will get treatment –

BB And Mr Joseph Duveen and Mr Bernard Berenson will make a large sum in profit –

Fowles A good deed isn't the less a good deed because everybody benefits. And actually, it won't be that large a sum – at least all the bids Joe's had so far have been less than he expected.

BB Well, that makes me feel much better. Thank you. Tell him if he can't get a decent bid – a decent bid – I'll find someone else who will.

Fowles Oh, I'm sure he'll get a decent bid. The lads will get their treatment, don't worry, BB.

BB looks at him suspiciously.

Fowles And we'll get our profit, don't worry, BB.

BB (*who has been studying him*) Tell me, Edward, do you enjoy your work?

Fowles I try to, BB, I think I do. The opportunities it gives me – it's given me –

BB To play golf at the weekends.

Fowles I enjoy my golf too. It keeps my mind off things. But it also concentrates it, if you follow me. That's the thing about golf – that you have to keep your eye, your mind, your muscles, your nerve all together in your wrist like a – a –

BB Botticelli?

Fowles What? Well, no. A golfer needs both wrists, you see, BB.

BB You play on Sundays?

Fowles Most Sundays, when I can.

BB I'd put you down as a man who went to church on Sundays.

Fowles Yes, I do that too.

BB (*nodding*) Church of England, then – golf and prayer on Sundays, and in service to Joseph Duveen for the rest of the week. Not much God but a hell of a lot of Mammon, I'd say. (*Smiles.*)

Fowles I take my religion seriously, BB. I consider it a privilege to work for Joe. I've never thought of it as being in service.

BB I'm teasing you, Fowles, teasing you. You don't usually take offence.

Fowles Oh, good heavens, I haven't taken offence, BB – oh, no thank you – (*refusing more wine*) – I've had quite enough – I know how you must feel, sometimes, it's difficult to be blessed with a gift that is so valuable to others. (*Reaches into his pocket.*) Oh, I've some photographs, by the way, Joe wants you to look at. (*Hands them to BB.*)

BB (*shuffles through them, giving each a fierce scrutiny*) A student's portfolio. School of Piedrelli, School of Gianticci, School of Ioniere, School of, School of – we have nothing of value here – what is this, this, what is this?

Fowles (*looks at photograph*) Well, that's the Pucerini, isn't it? Joe's had it cleaned.

BB Cleaned, cleaned, he's had it vandalised. Vandalised!

Fowles Well, you know the Americans, they like their masterpieces to look as fresh as paint.

BB I haven't seen it, I haven't seen it, make sure I haven't seen it or I shall have to speak about what I've seen.

Fowles Understood, BB. All Schools of, eh? Joe will be disappointed, he was hoping that at least a couple could be attributed –

BB Does that conclude our business?

Fowles There's one other matter – if I may mention it – Mellon is cutting up a bit about the Masaccio.

BB But he doesn't have a Masaccio. I thought I'd made that clear.

Fowles Yes, but when he bought it he thought he had. Joe told him he had. As it had been authenticated by you, BB.

BB I made a mistake.

Fowles He's returned it. He wants his money back.

BB Then he shall have to have it back, I expect.

Fowles But then you'll have to return your percentage.

BB (*after a little pause*) That of course is understood.

Fowles But if you were sure it was a Masaccio originally – Joe doesn't see why – it was a considered judgement, after all.

BB It is now a reconsidered judgement. I happened to look at it again. I saw that I'd been wrong. I never stick by my mistakes, Fowles, whatever the cost. What use would I be, with a damaged reputation? I'm beginning to develop a headache, perhaps we can continue with whatever needs continuing with after dinner.

Fowles Well, I'm not staying to dinner, BB, I tried to say to Miss Mariano –

BB But you're staying the night, aren't you? You have a room –

Fowles Oh, Mrs Berenson lent it to me for an hour, to lie down in – no, I'm back to Florence for the train. A flying visit. I've kept the driver –

BB Change your plans, send him away. Stay the night.

Fowles That's very kind of you, I wish I could, BB, but I told the immigration police, whatever they were –

BB Oh, good God, I'll deal with them.

Fowles And my wife is expecting me. It's her wedding anniversary.

BB Hers?

Fowles Ours I mean. We've never missed one.

BB Then give her my congratulations.

Fowles Thank you. And if Joe finds someone who will support your original authentication?

BB I shan't keep quiet. I shall challenge it. And of course, my word will be accepted. Because of my reputation. Explain that to Joe. And tell him if I can bear my losses, he can bear his. And I need the money and he doesn't. And tell him further – no, no, don't tell him anything further. I look forward to receiving what he owes me. (*Holds his hand out.*) Have a good trip back to hearth and home. Again, happy anniversary to Mrs Fowles. And yourself.

Fowles (*shaking his hand*) And my thanks to Mrs
Berenson and to Miss Mariano. Please make my
farewells for me. (*Leaves.*)

*BB stands for a moment, takes a few restless paces up
and down, sits down, pours himself a glass of wine,
takes a sip, grimaces as if finding it warm and sour,
flips the contents of the glass onto the grass.*

Lights.

SCENE TWO

*BB's library. Evening. BB is bent over a picture, examining
it with his magnifying glass. He is making notes, an image
of isolated concentration. A shaft of light, by which he is
working, is falling over his desk. In the alcove, Nicky is
working very rapidly through some bills. Mary is reading
under a small reading light in a corner.*

  *Mary turns a page, lets out a little laugh, which becomes
a slight groan. BB doesn't notice. Nicky looks towards
her. Mary glances at Nicky, smiles. Nicky smiles back.
Mary turns page, Nicky pretends to go back to work,
but keeps an eye on Mary. Mary stops reading, puts her
head back, then her hand to her stomach, clearly in pain.
Nicky gets up, goes across to her, puts her hand to
Mary's forehead.*

  Mary takes Nicky's hand away, gently holds it.

Nicky The doctor comes tomorrow. (*firmly*) I shall tell
Lizzie to send for him after breakfast.

Mary I don't think I need him.

Nicky Yes, you do.

Mary Very well then, I don't think I want him.

Nicky My dear, when it comes to your health you must think of others. It's not fair, is it, that we should be worried?

Mary looks at BB, whose intense concentration appears to make him deaf.

But he is. You know he is.

Mary Well then, he'll be far more worried if the doctor comes – there'll be a great deal of fuss and bother, which will be made entirely by him – (*nodding at BB*) – and then further fuss and bother at all the fuss and bother he's caused, and I shall get angry, which will make me feel sicker, and to what end, to be given more of the powders I'm already taking, and told to stay in bed until I feel able to get up, and perhaps I shan't feel able to get up ever again, you see?

Nicky (*in alarm*) No. What are you saying?

Mary I'm saying that I'm coming to know my sickness. Visits from the doctor, taking extra powders, staying a few days in bed make no difference to it whatsoever. They're merely distractions for me and you and him, but they don't distract it – (*slapping at her stomach*) – it goes on its own way, perfectly calmly and steadily, and will keep going on until it's finished its work.

Nicky But this is untrue! You have ups and downs, there are days, lots of days, when you're your old self.

Mary Darling Nicky, my old self is what I am becoming. What you're talking about is my younger self, my healthier self, which is not coming back.

BB lifts his head, stares at them. Mary and Nicky look at him. BB returns to his work, not having seen them.

I want everything to go on like this until Rachel and the grandchildren have visited.

Nicky But they're not here for another two weeks. Why not see the doctor so that you're at your best for them?

Mary (*sharply*) This is my best! That's what I'm telling you, Nicky. Now leave me alone, there's a good girl!

Nicky makes to protest.

(*sharply to Nicky as BB emerges from concentration*) Ssssh!

BB Well then, I'm ready.

Mary So we see. But what are you ready for?

BB Plato I think. Yes, Plato. The *Symposium*.

Mary But we did the *Symposium* just the other night.

BB No, we didn't, we scarcely started it. Then you got tired –

Mary Yes, well I'm a little tired again tonight. Too tired to read. I'd rather be read to. And nothing requiring thought. A novel.

BB Very well. But what? (*to Nicky*) You choose, my dear.

Nicky Well now . . . (*Thinks.*) It's a long time since we had Dickens. Or Jane Austen. What about *Mansfield Park*?

Mary Oh, too much morality. Bad for my dyspepsia. What about – what about – (*Checks a groan of pain.*) – something else?

Nicky (*glancing at her anxiously*) Well then – well then –

BB (*clapping his hands*) Come now, we're trying to organise some relaxation, let us be decisive.

Mary Did you have Inge, then?

BB Have Inge?

Mary For your massage.

BB Of course I didn't, you know I didn't, she was doing some football team, you told me yourself, why do you ask?

Mary You're so frisky. I always associate your bouts of friskiness with a massage. A physical liberation, I assume it to be.

BB We will read Hitler, I think. Yes. Hitler. *Mein Kampf*. (*to Nicky*) My dear, will you be the voice of our future?

Nicky (*after a little pause, firmly*) No, BB, I will not.

Mary I'd humour him if I were you. The tiger hasn't had his outing, he's on the prowl, and his claws are out. (*Going to BB, puts her hand on his head.*) Aren't they, BB?

BB Not a tiger, not even a cat, just a kitten. (*Takes her hand, kisses it.*) You know it.

Mary Well, a kitten of a tiger (*Kisses him on the top of the head, moves to the door. As she does so, picks up her decanter, exits.*)

BB She's going to drink herself to sleep, then.

Nicky Let's hope so. With that and a little opium – the pain is very bad.

BB We'll get the doctor over tomorrow.

Nicky She won't have him. I've already tried.

BB Then what are we to do?

Nicky She doesn't want us to do anything. Her only plan is to see her grandchildren again.

BB See her grandchildren, take to her bed, die. Is that it? (*Little pause.*) Does she know how I love her?

Nicky Of course she does. And don't worry about being disagreeable. She wouldn't have you any other way.

BB I don't know any other way, with her. It's as we've always been, right from the beginning. She had a husband and two children. She chose to abandon them for my sake. I am therefore responsible for her abiding sense of loss, her grief, her guilt. Which I much resent. *Voilà.*

Nicky She knows perfectly well that she abandoned her family for her own sake too, BB. She wanted what she knew you could make together.

BB Together!? Yes, yes, I don't deny it, can't deny it . . . She had the social gifts, the literary gifts. She introduced me to people we needed and taught me how to talk to them, how to be presentable. I may have had the eye, the instincts, the knowledge – the connoisseurship – but it was she that wrote them out for me, correcting my grammar, my punctuation, altering my vocabulary – making my work presentable. My Four Gospels presentable. It was a collaboration. A partnership. All my other collaborations and partnerships followed from that one. And now what is my life but a complication of partnerships? No, a conspiracy of partnerships, a collaboration of compromises –

Nicky BB! You don't hate her, you know.

BB Sometimes I do, Nicky.

Nicky But not now. Now is not the time.

BB Well, it seems to be, doesn't it? Because now she is bringing our long and fruitful and on my side childless collaboration to an end, and I find myself wishing –

Nicky Wishing what?

BB – that she and I had met as unattached man and woman, and then we might never have become attached, or if we had, simply become husband and wife to each other, and left it at that.

 Nicky laughs.

You find that funny?

Nicky Well, the idea that any couple could meet as man and woman, and then simply become husband and wife to each other, and leave it at that! Leave it at that! If only Adam and Eve had left it at that!

BB (*also laughing*) All right, then. If she'd found something else outside her marital duties –

Nicky Other than you?

BB Other than promoting me. Yes, she was my promoter. As if I were a – a boxer. That's what boxers have, I believe. Promoters.

Nicky From your previous complaints, I've always gathered that she had quite a lot to busy herself with outside her – her marital duties. As did you, after all.

BB Oh, adulteries! Our adulteries merely provided us with jealousy, which we both needed. Even then we had to transform it into sexual jealousy. It was really a profound irritation. Competitiveness. As one feels when a partner is dabbling in another enterprise. (*Stops.*) It is a contaminated love, that is what I am saying. But then mine is a contaminated life. In all its aspects.

Nicky Thank you. (*Little pause.*) And now would you like me to make love to you?

BB And would you?

Nicky Of course. That's how I keep my contamination healthy, you know. It grows by what it feeds on.

BB Do you still love me physically, then? At my age? And after so many years?

Nicky Oh, stop it, BB. You know I shall always love you. In all your aspects.

BB You've never, in all the years, shown a hint of jealousy. I don't think I'm altogether flattered by that.

Nicky You should be flattered by the fact that I've been completely faithful.

BB I couldn't have borne it if you hadn't been.

Nicky And yet you expect me to bear your infidelities. Even now. After so many years.

BB What do you mean? What infidelities? You can't mean the Swede. The sex is really just a part of her treatment. A massage with knobs on. (*Lets out a bark of surprised laughter.*)

Nicky looks at him.

Yes, well, you bring it out in me. It's one of your most delightful gifts.

Nicky When I first came here we spent hours together down here, you working so intensely, I watching you, learning how to help, I was so in love with you, and I knew you knew what I was feeling, you revelled in it, I could feel you revelling in it –

BB And so? They were wonderful hours, wonderful days, you've given me wonderful years, Nicky. I know that. I tell you so. More and more often. It's a form of dotage.

Nicky And so. And so. (*Pause.*) Every time you had a female house guest – I'd know whether you'd spent the night with her by Mary's little jokes in the morning. The only times I've ever hated her was when she made those jokes – she would watch my face as I tried to find an expression for her little jokes – you at least had the grace to dodge my look. I am not complaining, I am declaring my love. The nature of it. It has been well and truly tested, from the very beginning.

BB Poor Nicky. My poor Nicky.

Nicky Oh, I don't know. Look at us now. Having a merry old gossip about your old naughtiness – (*Kisses him.*)

BB – while upstairs my wife lies pining and dying.

Nicky That isn't what I was going to say.

BB Saying it doesn't make it better or worse.

Nicky That's always been one of your most curious mistakes. Saying things invariably makes them better or worse. Usually worse.

BB I don't agree. Not in these matters. In these matters I believe honesty a virtue. That's why I've insisted on it. In other matters – in my life's work, for instance – I have avoided it at all costs. At all costs. As Mary knows. As Joe knows. As even little Mr Fowles knows.

Nicky I won't have it, BB. (*Puts her finger to his lips.*) No anger tonight.

BB It wasn't going to be anger, it was going to be spite. And only against myself.

Nicky Well, I won't have you being spitely, not even against yourself. Especially against yourself.

BB Spitely! (*delighted*) That's the first mistake I've heard you make in three years.

Nicky But I've heard the word. I've heard it often. Mary uses it of you. 'Well, BB is very spitely this morning. He's back to his spitely best.'

BB She says 'sprightly', meaning vigorous, alive, etc. And all the time you thought she meant spiteful, did you? 'BB's back to his spiteful best, he's very spiteful this morning.' Well, perhaps she did, come to think of it. Come here, please.

   Nicky goes to him.

(*Takes her hand, presses it into his crotch.*) There. You see. Sprightly.

Nicky So you have been arousing yourself, that's what you've been doing, with all this spitefulness against yourself. To make yourself feel more manly, is that it, BB? (*kissing him*)

BB Well, perhaps I've been searching for a touch of manliness in myself, yes. Honour often comes with it, I believe.

Nicky Let me tell you something, BB, let me tell you what I always think when you talk badly about yourself. (*Kneels beside him.*)

BB I know what you always think.

Nicky Well, listen again. You've taught people how to look at a painting and see all the subtleties of colour, of shape and form – you've taught them how to see light and shade and most of all – most of all –

BB – most of all I've taken them into the very soul of the artist!

Nicky Well, you have.

BB That's one of the things I don't say to myself. What is it I take into the very souls of the artists, Nicky, may I ask? Now it's true that because of me Mr John Pierpoint Morgan, and Mr Frick and Mr Henry Huntingdon own Pieros and Botticellis and Amici di Sandro, and hang them in their private residences and their galleries and add them to their great collections, but where are the souls of these men, do you think? Do they dwell in the souls of the artists I help them acquire? And why do you think they have souls at all – and furthermore why do you think artists great or otherwise have souls? The word is part of the patter of the museum guides. It is scarcely off the lips of Joe Duveen when he is attempting to effect one of his sales – 'Here, come and look at this, what am I offered for this, how much for this great picture in which the wonderful soul of the magnificent artist is at its most beautifully blossoming? Here, here is a document signed by the Great Expert and Connoisseur Bernard Berenson himself, whose soul has been right into the soul of our most divine artists, and who now authenticates that this is the best soul available on the market at these prices. You can hang it on one of your walls and let your soul enter its soul for a million and a half dollars – yes, a mere million and a half dollars, which means only the smallest profit for me of sixty-five hundred and don't forget I have to take out a ten per cent commission for the Great Expert and Connoisseur for allowing us the use of his soul to take us on a guided tour around the soul of this great and wonderful and magnificent artist!'

Nicky So what word would you use, then, if not soul?

BB I have an eye (*pointing to it*) that can see. A brain (*tapping it*) that can think. A memory (*wagging his hand* *over his face)* that can connect. I have no soul. It is not only the word that disgusts me. It is the very thought of the thing itself. It distracts attention from man's achievement, which is that he has evolved from the slime without benefit of soul. He has only his natural faculties and his determination to cultivate them. No soul. No God. Just this, this, and that. *(pointing to his eyes, his heart and face)*

Nicky And yet all the work you love so deeply, to which you've given your life, what is it but a celebration of the love of God, and where does that come from but the soul?

BB This isn't a conversation between a man and his mistress, it's a debate between a Lithuanian Jewish atheist and a Slav-Italian Catholic. How perfectly matched we are.

Nicky I've seen you a thousand times looking at a painting. Your face – your face has been full of soul, my darling.

BB Why not say 'my child'? All that you have seen is an intelligent man concentrating in wonder and gratitude on the creative powers of fellow members of the human race.

Nicky Who believed that God gave them their creative powers, their – *(Nods.)*

BB Their creative powers gave them their God and their souls. Now we are grateful for the metaphors they give to us.

Nicky As a child – in Lithuania – when you used to wander about in the woods – what you described, the way you've described it –

BB I described a child in the woods, suddenly seeing the light. I saw the light. With my eyes. Just as now, if I were

to look out of the window, I would see darkness. And
one day soon, we will see the darkness in the light.
One morning or afternoon, in the sunshine, there will
be the Duck quacking at our gates. Not the devil, but the
monster Duck. And then however bright the sun, we will
be living in an eclipse, a man-made eclipse, another
human achievement to wonder at. Again without benefit
of soul. Quack, quack. Where are you going?

Nicky I'm going to bed.

BB Are you angry with me?

Nicky Of course not. But I'm a little tired of you.

BB Tired of me!

Nicky By, I meant. A prepositional error, BB. Tired by
your vitality this evening. Besides, it's time I looked in on
Mary.

BB And may I wake you when I've done my turn?

Nicky Of course you may. (*Smiles at him, goes out.*)

> BB *gets up, walks restlessly about, plucking books
> down, glancing into them, replacing them impatiently,
> goes to a folio of drawings, stops at one, studies it
> closely, then turns to another, then another. He lifts
> his head suddenly, listening, as if he's caught a faint
> sound. Studies the folio, puts it down, exasperated
> and impatient.*

BB What, what, what! There's something missing,
there's always something missing.

> *There is a loud knock on the door. BB swivels
> towards it, bewildered. There is another brutal knock.*

(*belligerently, defiantly*) Who is it, what do you want?

The door opens. Duveen enters. He is magnificently dressed, or appears to be, from what is visible of his clothes – bottom of trousers, shoes, etc. He is wearing his usual hat, a silk scarf, a flower in his buttonhole, an astrakhan coat, top hat in hand. BB lets out a laugh of incredulity.

Duveen Happy birthday, BB.

BB Thank you. How did you get in? Through the window?

Duveen I rang the bell, of course. Quietly, so as not to disturb Mary. I hear that she's been unwell, I'm sorry. What's the matter with her?

BB She has a problem with her digestion, nothing for you to bother yourself about – and who let you in?

Duveen Your enchanting Miss Mariano. She said you'd just been talking about the devil, so perhaps you were expecting me. She makes such nice jokes and she has such a smile – how I envy you, BB, to have such a smile in the house. (*Holds out his arms.*) Come here.

BB Why?

Duveen So that I can embrace you. Fold you in my arms.

BB Why?

Duveen To say happy birthday.

BB It's not my birthday.

Duveen I intend to make you feel that it is. That every day from now to the end of your life is your birthday. (*waggling his arms*) Come, BB!

BB (*laughs in spite of himself*) I will not.

Duveen You see – even the simplest gesture of affection – you spurn me, BB. Spurn me. And I've travelled a long way, tired myself out, by car, train, boat, train, car, all the way here just to make peace with you.

BB Ah well, Joe – if you want to make peace – (*moving towards him*)

  Duveen throws his arms out again.

(*skipping nimbly around him*) – you can begin by settling our accounts.

Duveen Our accounts need settling?

BB You know they do.

Duveen But hasn't my Edward Fowles been, from my Paris office? I sent him orders to do that, exactly that, he was to settle our accounts, down to the last halfpenny, sou and cent. Those were my exact words, halfpenny, sou and cent, he was under specific instruction not to take his leave of you until it had all been agreed – was it not agreed, then, BB? He sent me messages saying that it was. He was lying to me then, but why should he lie, Edward Fowles? He knows you, admires you, worships you, he'd do anything – he's almost my adopted son, did you know he started as a lift boy? Yes, but he was so attentive to the conversations of his passengers as he took them up and down, down and up, passed the relevant details on so assiduously that I identified him immediately as a member of the family, an associate member, tucked him under my wing – and now you say he has been lying, lying to me, BB, then God help us all!

BB I didn't say he'd been lying, in fact he quite evidently hasn't been lying if he said we'd agreed on the sum you owed me, the point is that this sum hasn't arrived, Joe, it's still outstanding, to the inconvenience of the household.

Duveen Ah, well that's a relief then. That I should have had doubts about my Edward, what happens to us as we get on in life, BB. It's not in my nature to doubt the intentions of any man, but what I find, you know, what I find is that I understand men less and less, even the simplest ones, I know more and more what they will do, less and less why they will do it. Here, listen to this, BB, bear with me, just the other day I offered the man from Pennsylvania a beautiful painting, a marvellous and original, a great painting by a great but unknown master at a bargain price, fifty thousand dollars, fifty thousand dollars! That isn't a sale, it is a gift, but he said no, no, I will not pay fifty thousand dollars, on any account. So, scarcely believing his folly, his insolence, I try again, and I say forty thousand dollars, no, he says, in contempt, please don't bother me any more with this – this almost valueless piece of canvas, and so now it is a challenge, I ask myself what will I do to make him buy this painting, I of course know what I will do, and you – you know too, BB – I will wait six months, will I not? and then I will come back to him and say of the painting, this same painting, I have decided to let you have it for one hundred and fifty thousand dollars, and this time it is he who will look thoughtful, troubled, he will hesitate, and I will say, furthermore you will have to pay all the costs of storage and removal and furthermore you will have to pay for a copy to replace it in the private collection from which it is being sold and furthermore you will have to pay me a double commission for the impertinence of not buying it when I first offered it to you, and furthermore I may not sell it to you anyway, I may decide that you are not a worthy owner, and then of course he will hesitate and worry no longer, on the spot, he will give me the hundred and fifty thousand dollars along with various other thousands for my expenses. That is an absolute fact, known to me, known to you, too, BB, but not so far known to him. And yet for you, BB, as for me, a mystery, not what I will do and what he will do, but how do I know what he will do, and why he will do it.

BB You know both answers perfectly well, Joe. You started by offering him a cheap picture, now you're going to let him have a valuable one, one that in a few months has leapt in price by a hundred and ten thousand dollars – in a few more months he'll be able to sell it on to one of his collector friends for two hundred thousand, from whom, perhaps, you'll buy it back to sell on for half a million, etc., etc. That's how you promote your masterpieces into the world, you haggle them in. I've seen you at it, remember. On a number of occasions. When I introduced you to Lord Allendale, you plonked yourself in front of his Rembrandt and you – you – haggled. (*Gestures contemptuously.*)

Duveen Haggled! I did no such thing, quite the contrary, I did exactly the reverse 'Hello, here is a Rembrandt, HERE IS A REMBRANDT, and my God what a Rembrandt this is, one of the five greatest pictures ever painted, no, four, one of the four – three – three most magnificent – My Lord, I will give you seventy-five, no, eighty – no, no, Joe! for this most sublime – look at the face, the nose, the nose is worth a fortune in itself, I'd give you a fortune for your Rembrandt's nose, Lord A, and for the whole face I would empty my coffers, a hundred and twenty-five, a hundred and eighty – you name the price, my dear Lord A, whisper a sum and there'll be a runner with a cheque for twice the amount on your doorstep by dawn.' How can you call that haggling, BB?

BB (*enjoying the memory in spite of himself*) No, no, you're quite right, you were auctioning – you were auctioning his Rembrandt in his own living room to

35

yourself. I was astonished he didn't throw you out of the house.

Duveen That was because you didn't understand him. He adored it, having a noisy Jew shouting prices at him in an ecstasy of acquisitiveness. He didn't expect it of a Jew. Such Jewishness. He expected a creeper and bower and a mutterer, a man ashamed of money – do you know what he said to me when I left? He said, 'I'll promise you this, Duveen, if I ever decide to sell, you're the man I'll sell to.' And six months later he did decide, I was the man. I am still a frequent guest at his dinner parties. (*Beams proudly at BB.*) Oh, it's good to be here again, in I Tatti – after only a few minutes I feel its influence seeping through the pores of my skin.

BB Good. And now perhaps back to the question of the money you owe me.

Duveen But we have never left it, BB. That is what we're discussing, all the time. That. And more than that. Much is at stake here for both of us, believe me.

BB What?

Duveen Let me come to it, BB, in my own way. It's been such a long time that we've stood together in the same room – most particularly in your room – need I stand, by the way? My back –

BB You may take a chair, if you wish.

Duveen And so we need a little time together, to talk in the way that we used to – (*sitting down*)

BB We didn't talk, Joe. We squabbled. We often ended up shouting into each other's faces. Once or twice I found myself on the verge of hitting you. As you know, I detest violence.

Duveen You mustn't blame only yourself, BB. There were flashes of intemperance on my part, too. You know, it's really because we're so fond of each other. For thirty years we've been colleagues, friends, brothers – yes, brothers, and, like brothers, so much in common, so many differences – you a Lithuanian Jew of impoverished background, a self-made American aristocrat, I a Dutch Jew second-generation Englishman, completely uneducated though born to wealth – the family fortune founded on the talents of a peddler who traded in lard, pig's fat –

BB I know our biographies, Joe. Yours almost as well as mine, as I've heard you tell it so often.

Duveen But not always the same version, I hope. I like to think I adapt the details to suit the audience. In New York, I find in myself the English aristocrat, in London Lord Allendale's American Jew –

BB stirs impatiently.

(*quickly*) But with you, BB, even when we're at logger-heads, shouting into each other's faces as you put it, like brothers, I feel outclassed. It is humiliating.

BB Oh come, Joe, there is nothing that you find humiliating. It is your great strength.

Duveen I used the wrong word. It should have been 'humbled'. Your gifts humble me. They have always humbled me.

BB Only because you needed them to make money.

Duveen Ah yes, ah yes – there it is. That is the real difficulty between us. The truth is that you are ashamed of me, BB. You feel demeaned by our association. You think I peddle great pictures to barbarians to serve my own interests, but I tell you this, I have awakened something in these barbarians – in Huntington, in Mellon, in

37

Frick – in Kress – something that all their millions never brought them before. Until I came into their lives these men thought they had everything the world could give them, that God had rewarded them to the limit for their years of slavish devotion to self-betterment.

BB (*laughing*) Oh stop, Joe, stop it, God, self-betterment – Frick, Morgan, Mellon! Their God is Mammon, their self-betterment is in getting richer and richer.

Duveen No, BB, no, no – you either gaze closely into the soul of things or you look down from your loftiness, either way you fail to see all those of us who live in the middle distance.

BB The middle distance? And that is what I have the sensation of sinking into, is it, at this moment, the middle distance? It has a powerful stench, this middle distance of yours, and your voice calling out from it has an oink-oink.

Duveen You should be ashamed of yourself, BB.

BB For insulting you?

Duveen For being so simple in your insults. Frick, Mellon, Kress – they're not pigs, for whom, by the way, you should have a more tender regard. Pigs are enchanting creatures, of considerable intelligence, capable of warmth and great loyalty – which is no doubt why Christians breed, kill and eat them.

BB They breed and kill them so that they can eat pork and bacon. Why – why are we talking about pigs, anyway? You haven't come here to discuss farming or the eating habits of Christians, you've come here to pay your debt and discuss some arrangement, so you said, and here we are in pigs – and how typical of you to reduce a figure of speech to its literal content and then lure me into one of your squabbles. Go away! Send back the lift boy, he has ten times your conversational dignity. Go on, off with you, off, off!

Duveen Really, BB, you make me sound like an old horse! Nevertheless you are offended. (*Bows.*) I apologise.

BB Yes, yes, so you should – well, perhaps it's not entirely your fault, the trouble is, Joe, I don't trust you – especially when you're being pious.

Duveen If I had your education –

BB – you would be without your main weapon, which is your lack of it.

Duveen Your intelligence, then.

BB looks at him.

Again my apologies. I was merely attempting to explain – explain? I'm merely trying to explain to you that Frick, Mellon and Kress aren't merely gross capitalists, they come from religious backgrounds, they believe in goodness and virtue –

BB – they exploit their fellow human beings. They pay them almost nothing, work them to early graves –

Duveen Well, that is what is meant by the Protestant work ethic, their success is the mark of their salvation. Their employees' misery is the mark of *their* damnation. It is the American way. Joyless power, fruitless wealth – salvation. Grinding poverty, hopeless misery – damnation. The afterlife is eternal and merciless capitalism.

BB Ah, I see. And the paintings you sell them, all the great works of the Renaissance, are making Catholics of them, are they? You are teaching them the joys of power, the fruitfulness of money, how to be libertines, even?

Duveen Oh no, I don't want them to be libertines. If they were libertines they wouldn't spend on great art, they'd spend on women, boys, guardsmen, horses –

BB Oh, they'd have enough money for all that, and art too.

Duveen Yes, but not the time. You see. That's it. These millionaire collectors, men like Frick, Mellon and Kress, are single-minded, obsessive and puritanical. They take their art very seriously. Why, do you remember Henry Huntington, and what he did to the delicious Mrs Siddons, the subtlest, the most gorgeous portrait Sir Joshua Reynolds ever painted – when he discovered she, this noble beauty, wasn't a society lady after all, merely an actress and therefore, therefore a whore, he had her taken down from his wall and – (*Makes a chucking out gesture.*)

BB In fact he had her transferred to the city gallery. I have heard you cite the story as an illustration of Henry Huntington's public-spirited munifence.

Duveen Exactly, exactly, hung her out so that her charms could be inspected by *tout le monde*, like a whore, like the whore he thought she was, you're quite right, BB, that's my very point, a whore! (*Gives a loud laugh, slightly odd.*) But why was I – Mrs Siddons – oh yes. Beauty. Not the whore, Mrs Siddons, but beauty – beauty must be virtuous, not only expensive but virtuous, for Frick, for Mellon and Kress. Also, of course, it must be in the market place, where they can understand it in their usual currency. So it was with Huntington, so it has been with Frick, Mellon, Kress.

BB Frick, Mellon and Kress, Frick, Mellon and Kress – you keep bringing them in together as if they are a circus troupe. Who is Kress?

Duveen Kress is Mr Five-and-Dime. He owns a chain of them, across America, buys everything in bulk very cheap – no, he buys *anything* in bulk as long as it's very cheap, and sells it for one cent, two cents more –

BB In other words he's a store-keeper. Like yourself.

Duveen (*stares at him*) What do you mean?

BB I mean that you keep a store. Like Kress.

Duveen A store! A store! (*Laughs.*) I have constructed one of the most elegant buildings in New York – in the very heart of Manhattan recreated a glory of Parisian architecture and in this – this palace I house one of the world's most beautiful collections of art – why, in my basement, my basement, sir, there are Goyas and – and – (*Stops, stares at BB, bewildered.*)

BB You've forgotten.

Duveen What? What?

BB Where you are, who you're talking to.

Duveen I'm talking to you, BB. (*Gathers himself.*) What do you mean, who am I talking to, BB? I'm talking to you, of course!

BB You're all right then? For a moment I thought we were going to lose you.

Duveen I'm here, I'm here, exactly where I intended to be, lose me, hah! Now what was I talking to you about? You've distracted me.

BB You were talking about your shop – no, sorry – your emporium in Manhattan, in the basement of which you keep stored beautiful works of art which you hope are going up in price with every passing month, like wines and some cheeses. If you didn't follow it, don't worry,

you didn't miss anything, it was just your usual patter –
but there's something missing. Something – (*Gestures,
then identifies his gestures.*) Oh, of course. Your cigar.
Where's your cigar?

Duveen Cigar? Oh yes – the doctors forbid. But I keep
one about me – for a festive occasion – (*fumbling in his
pocket*) – times like these – (*Stops fumbling, mumbles
something, the word 'devil' just audible.*)

BB What? What did you say?

Duveen Mmm?

BB About the devil. You said something about the devil,
I didn't quite hear it.

Duveen The devil, eh, the devil, did I, well, I probably
said let him take the hindmost, eh, BB? (*Roars out an
odd laugh, stops it abruptly, stares at BB.*)

BB Joe? (*Little pause.*) Joe?

Duveen (*starting into sudden fluency*). Yes, there he is,
was sitting in a café in Algeria –

BB Who?

Duveen Kress, Samuel Kress, King of the Five-and-Dime,
and along comes one of those street traders – (*Imitates.*)
– shawls, shawls, beautiful shawls – pushing them along
in his handcart – so Kress calls him over, has a look at
one of these shawls, quite a good shawl, not a bad
shawl, a street trader's shawl but of a quality, so he
looks at his lady friend, and she shakes her head, why
would a woman sitting next to millions want him to buy
a street trader's shawl? No, she's not interested, she's got
shawls from India, China, Turkey, all bought in Fifth
Avenue or Harrods, why should she want a shawl from
Algiers in Algiers when she can get it at five times the

price in Fifth Avenue, Harrods? She's a big woman, by
the way, loves hats, enormous hats, if you threw one
of her hats into the ring you couldn't have the fight, so
she's no to the shawls, wants the street trader and his
handcart sent on his way, but there's something about
this street trader and his shawls, a cunning in the eyes,
a guile in the mouth, this street trader, so our man, he
can't let the opportunity slip by, even in a café in Algiers
on his holiday, with a trader who trades he has to trade
a little, what else is there for him to do, with his giant
lady friend heaving away beside him, the sun beating
down, the clamour of the market – so he begins, how
much are they? Ah, and in dollars how much? Ah, and if
he pays dollars now how much? Ah, and if he buys two
shawls now how much in discount, and the discount for
three how much, how much, say, if he buys half the
stock he sees before him, would he get a couple from the
half he leaves behind thrown in free, ah, and how much
for three quarters of the stock, what discount, how many
thrown in free from the quarter he leaves behind, ah,
and now suppose he buys the whole stock he sees before
him, what discount, ah, but then what about the number
that would have been thrown in free if he'd left any
behind, how does that affect the discount, does he get
a bigger discount, ah, and how many shawls does this
trader have apart from what's on his hand-barrow, ah,
well then put that stock on top of this stock how much
discount? So on it goes and on, until at the end, the big
lady friend long gone back to her hotel, he makes his
purchase there in the café in Algiers of seven thousand
and three hundred and fifty shawls of which two
hundred and fifty are completely free, another two
thousand and one hundred and fifty shawls discounted
down to almost their true worth, the deal of a lifetime,
even when he's paid to ship them back to his New Haven
warehouse and then paid to have them distributed to

a hundred or so selected outlets, because when he's sold every single one of them, which he will do, he'll have made a clear profit of three hundred and forty-eight dollars, which will be a seventy per cent profit, that's it, you see, that's the point, for this man of many millions, he will have pulled off a remarkable coup of a seventy per cent profit, who cares whether it's in millions or in cents, that's what matters to him, that's the spirit of him.

BB And now he's buying his shawls from you.

Duveen He tries. I kept him away for five years, but let him know, by this way and that way, how my dealings with Mellon were proceeding. He worships Mellon. For him Mellon is aristocracy, just as for Mellon, Frick was aristocracy. So I nursed him with stories of how Duveen had permitted Mellon to make this great purchase and that Duveen had granted Mellon the privilege of spending many hundreds of thousands on the Piero della Francesca – groomed Mellon, you see, into a man worthy of his purchases. So how could I not fail with Kress the worshipper of Mellon, the aspiring aristocrat? So it was with great faith, faith above all in my own power to educate – to *educate* – that I led him gently through the sacred chambers of my gallery, scarcely allowing him to pause until we reached a shrine. Amico di Sandro. (*Nods at BB.*) So you had designated it, BB. I folded my hands, so. (*Folds them.*) And gestured thus. (*Gestures prayerfully with his hands.*) And he looked at this – this truly – of a grace, a charm, a religious tenderness, of a holiness and a lustrousness – as I said to him. Whispered to him. Holiness. Lustrousness. (*whispering intently*) Luminousness. And he stared at it – he has a squint when he's concentrating – he squinted at it for eight, nine, ten seconds, and he said, 'How much?' I doubled the largest sum that came into my head and added fifty thousand. He said, those two rooms back there, the ones

44

we came through, there were six paintings in each room, who were they by? Well, I said, there were two Titians, a Gainsborough, a Tintoretto, a Botticelli and an Ucello. And how much were those, he asked? Well, I said, and I began to give him the price of each. Ah, he said, but if I bought the lot. And I named a price, a price, I named a price, a sum, a huge one – ah, he said, now if I bought this masterpiece here and three in there, what kind of discount would you give me? And if I only took three but with the masterpiece here? Ah, and now if I took five and the masterpiece, ah, and if I took all six and the masterpiece, what would you throw in free, and what discount on all six,? And so – and so – I found myself becoming the street trader in Algiers, I began to trade, yes, before I knew it, no, no, I shouted, no, no, these are not for sale, none of these is for sale, not to you, they're already sold, they're going to Mr Mellon. Oh, Mr Mellon, he said, well, why didn't you just say so in the first place? Because I've only just realised, I said, and I haven't told Mr Mellon yet. Well, how do you know he'll buy them, he said. Because, I said, because I'll tell him that if he doesn't they'll go to you. Ah, he said. Ah. He didn't say another word except goodbye and thank you when I shook him by the hand on the pavement. Now I'm beginning to allow him some droppings from my table, but you know the story about the appetite, and what it feeds on. And with Frick dead, Mellon dying –

BB Mellon dying?

Duveen But not dead. Not yet dead. We can't have him dead until he's finished his life's work, on which his immortality depends. A few works for him still to acquire. And then he may go. In peace and triumph. With one of the world's greatest collections as his memorial. (*Looks at BB, an odd and challenging look.*) Well, we're all in quest of immortality of some kind of another – otherwise

we wouldn't be mere mortals, would we, BB? Of course
we can't help seeing the bogusness of it, can we? What
makes us immortal, Frick, Mellon, and no doubt Kress
in his turn – and me, come to think of it, with my rooms
at the Tate, and the National – is the immortal achievements of others. That people will hurry eagerly to the
Frick and the Mellon and my rooms and wings not to
see the work of Frick or Mellon or myself, merely the
acquisitions of Frick and Mellon and myself – all our
grubbing and greed and ambition transformed into the
tenderest, most graceful, the truly sublime achievements
of men who died in poverty and obscurity. Think of
Rembrandt, think of Caravaggio – of Giorgione, Titian
even – and where are they? Housed in the Frick, the
Mellon, eventually the Kress, my rooms and wings
bringing lustre and immortality –

BB You are about to lose your trusteeship. Did you
know that?

Duveen What? (*Stares at him.*) What do you mean?

BB Your trusteeship of the National Gallery. You're
about to lose it.

Duveen It is gossip and rumour. Nothing has been settled.
It'll become evident when they consider it properly that
my relationship with the Gallery is completely *comme
il faut*.

BB My understanding is that you were behind several of
its important purchases, and that your position has
therefore become untenable.

Duveen I was in a position to bring certain items to the
Gallery that have added to its prestige. The Sassetta
panels, for instance. I could have put them on the
commercial market to far greater profit to myself.

46

BB Ah well, in England, you know, the *appearance* of impropriety is the impropriety. You would have understood that if you hadn't spent so much time in America. You've got into the habit of thinking of yourself as a sort of king, a position only tenable nowadays in a capitalist democracy. And when you come to England and go to Allendale's house and play the buffoon –

Duveen I behave as I believe. That all men are born equal.

BB That is what I mean by buffoon. And they love you for it, or so you like to boast – your enthusiasm, your vulgarity, your patter of money and so forth – and that is why you'll lose your trusteeship.

Duveen Never. They wouldn't – they couldn't – I've done too much for them, I've given and given – great rooms at the Tate, the National, entirely funded by me.

BB But you've left them nothing to put in them. You've sold all their great paintings to America in order to pro- vide them with wings and rooms named after yourself. You've already got your memorials – why do you care about the trusteeship?

Duveen To bring back some of the treasures that belong – belong – with the Sassetta panels I will lose money! Yes, probably lose money. And certainly time and energy, which I should be hoarding. At my time of life hoarding my time, my money! I have done nothing wrong! (*He is shaking, sits down.*) Nothing wrong! It is a sacred trust, to be a trustee –

BB Yes, yes – a sacred trust. Not to be bought or sold, you see, Joe, not like your knighthood or your peerage – those are decorations, to be dispensed as rewards by this or that passing government – but the National Gallery is at the heart of the matter. Not an honour and a privilege, but a duty, Joe, you see. By buying and selling even on their behalf, and for their advantage, you've shown that you're a mere tradesman in your soul, they realise they've been letting you enter and leave by the wrong door.

Duveen (*rallying*) I shall sort it out. I shall dispose of the panels somewhere else, by the time they get into the Gallery my name will no longer be attached to them.

BB I doubt that your name will still be attached to the trusteeship.

Duveen They need me.

BB They needed you.

Duveen I'll tell you what is odd, BB – that of the two of us, the scholar and the tradesman, it is you that should be the cynic.

BB It saves one a great deal of disappointment.

Duveen The question for you, BB, is what your name will be attached to, when you've gone.

BB I am quite content to leave my writings, There are some writings, I believe, among them four books on Renaissance painting which people are kind enough to refer to as the Four –

Duveen – Gospels, an unmatchable achievement, unmatchable, sublime, but as great, as full, perhaps an even fuller expression of yourself – well, we're sitting in it, BB, I Tatti – your collection, your library, your gardens, the views – here, if anywhere, the spirit of you, your sense of beauty, the delicacy and humanity – the fineness of perception – the all-creating eye –

BB You're fluting, Joe.

Duveen Fluting, fluting, how can I be fluting, I'm making a deal?

BB In your special Heavenly Choir voice, which means that something unsavoury is in the offing. There's only one deal you can make with me –

Duveen You want the money I owe you, I told you, I have brought it with me. (*Takes cheque out of pocket.*) You want I Tatti to remain as it is long after your death. I can provide the means of doing so. Even Harvard will be grateful. The real reason I come here tonight by train, boat, car – I'd have come on camel or on foot if I'd had to – I have come to offer you a partnership, BB.

BB A partnership?

Duveen A full partnership. Now come on. (*holding out his arms*)

BB hesitates.

Colleague, friend, brother, partners. Full partners. Now what squabbles we'll have, eh? (*wagging his arms*) Come. Don't be churlish. I'm giving you your immortality. Eh, my BB!

BB allows Duveen to wrap his arms around him. They stand, embracing.

Lights.

Act Two

The same. Two seconds later.

BB (*separates himself from Duveen*) A full partnership?

Duveen A full partnership.

BB That would mean, in my understanding, that would mean that I would receive a percentage on any transaction you completed, whether I participated in it or not?

Duveen Yes. That is what it means. That is the full meaning of full partnership.

BB But I assume that my commissions on any transactions that came your way through my – influence – would remain as they are.

Duveen Well, of course.

BB And if I ceased to interest myself in any such transactions –

Duveen Ah. But why should you?

BB Well, the present political situation, the impending war – and there are family concerns – Mary's family, needless to say? (*little laugh*) It may be that I have to retire from direct involvement. Well, who knows the reasons? To tell you the truth, my health – my reputation too – I find increasingly that the state of my health depends on the state of my reputation.

Duveen Well, that is good, BB, very good. Your reputation has never been so high. There should be colour in your cheeks. A good colour.

BB You haven't answered my question, Joe.

Duveen Your question?

BB Whether I would retain my partnership if I ceased to involve myself in transactions –

Duveen You would have to waive your commission.

BB Well, of course! I could scarcely claim a commission on transactions I hadn't undertaken.

Duveen Of course not. (*Laughs.*) Any more than you could undertake transactions without claiming a commission.

BB By which you mean?

Duveen No independent transactions. No deals with other dealers. In other words.

BB And if there were no deals at all?

Duveen shrugs.

But I would retain my partnership?

Duveen Such is your value, BB.

BB How gratifying.

Duveen And if you decide to involve yourself directly in any deal, your commission would be increased. As befits a full partner.

BB By how much.

Duveen It would be doubled. It would become fifteen per cent.

BB Doubled would be twenty per cent.

Duveen Doubled, I mean, from when we first entered into our arrangement.

BB No, from when we last nearly terminated it.

Duveen You see.

BB See what?

Duveen How helpless you always make me feel. There should be such a simple opposition, the trader and man of the world dealing with the scholar and recluse – you should have no chance with me at all, and yet I end up yielding everything, everything.

BB The value of my name has depended on its not being publicly connected to yours. Our partnership must not be allowed to affect that.

Duveen You mean you wish our partnership to be confidential?

BB Of course.

Duveen So that your authentications will retain their integrity?

BB Of course.

Duveen But you will continue to authenticate?

BB Of course.

Duveen Well, that all seems clear and above board.

BB And it will be. I have no intention of letting our partnership compromise my authentications. They will be authentic.

Duveen I for one have never questioned your integrity. Although being occasionally human, you've made occasional mistakes, wouldn't you agree?

BB I've never considered it a matter of honour to stand by my mistakes. I've confessed to quite a few embarrassments in my time.

Duveen You have. And sometimes the greater embarrassment has been mine. Retracting your authentication of Bellini cost me half a million dollars.

BB It brought you more in reputation.

Duveen Who knows? There's no price can be put on honour, as Shakespeare said. Was it Shylock?

BB You may be thinking of Falstaff, who said honour had no price because it was worthless.

Duveen Did he say that? Then he must have been down on his luck, eh?

BB (*after a little pause*) I accept.

Duveen opens his arms again.

May we do it my way this time, Joe? (*Offers his hand.*)

Duveen takes it. They shake.

Duveen Well then. That concludes – that seems to conclude – I can go home – (*picking up hat and stick*) – with everything settled between us. Settled at last. (*Stares at BB. Moved.*)

BB Apart that is, for the – (*Makes a little gesture, with his finger.*)

Duveen I think you'll find it in your pocket.

BB looks at him, feels in his pocket, takes out cheque, laughs.

You see what comes when you cuddle your partner?

BB I wish you bon voyage, Joe. And a good war.

Duveen We will proceed as if there isn't going to be one. And then as if there isn't one going on. And then – will you be safe?

BB I'm an American.

Duveen An American Jew.

BB The American will look after the Jew.

Duveen The world of art, of the human spirit, that owes you so much, will look after both of you, BB.

BB (*moved*) Thank you. Thank you, Joe.

Duveen My love to Mary. Tell her her health comes first. And the enchanting Miss Mariano I shall doubtless see at the door, when she lets me out.

BB Perhaps you'll ask her to look in on me. And allow me the pleasure of breaking the news to her myself.

Duveen As long as she allows me one of her smiles . . .

> *They look at each other. Duveen makes to say something else, goes to door.*

BB And love to – love to – (*as Duveen exits*) Dollie and – (*Gestures. Stands for a moment, almost bewildered.*) Well. Well then. Like a hallucination. Let's trust not, let's trust not.

> *Looks at the cheque, clearly scrutinises the amount, nods in satisfaction, goes to Nicky's desk, puts cheque carefully on it, then in spite of himself cuts a little caper.*
> *Door opens. Duveen enters, carrying a shiny large oblong case, in black leather, with a handle, a form of briefcase.*

Duveen I left it outside your door. In my excitement I nearly walked right past it, out, into the night.

BB What is it?

Duveen Ah! (*Raises a finger, looks around, sees a stand, on which there is a picture underneath a light, which is* *off.*) May I? (*Turns on light, looks at picture as he removes it from stand.*) Goya. But I thought you detested Goya.

BB That's why I keep it in the dark. Except when I am studying it. I'm thinking of writing a short paper – no, not there – put it there. (*indicating a corner*)

Duveen places the Goya where BB indicated, adjusts stand for best visibility, goes to his case, takes a bunch of keys out of his pocket, uses a succession of keys to open case, each clicking, opens lid ceremonially, takes picture out. Carries it to the stand, arranges it there, steps away. BB watches, then turns away, indifferent.

Duveen It is *The Adoration of the Shepherds*!

BB laughs.

Well, don't you want to look?

BB At a copy, why should I look at a copy when I carry the original in my head?

Duveen smiles.
    BB, almost in spite of himself, turns, glances at painting, almost turns away, stops himself, goes to painting, studies it briefly.

Good God, Joe, you've been carrying this in your luggage – in cars, boats – (*Gestures.*)

Duveen Just that you might have a look at it, yes, BB – it travelled very expensively, every customs official between Florence and Paris has been able to treat his wife and mistresses to a splendid meal. It made me think of the old days, BB, when Mary had the false bottoms to her suitcases and that trunk – and her hat-boxes for the icons – how is the light, perhaps still not at the right angle – (*Goes to adjust it.*)

BB, who is looking at the painting, gestures impatiently.

Then you have it. In all its glory, reverence – you can see the brush-strokes, the details? And the whole – you can take in the whole – is it not beautiful?

BB It is most beautiful. It has always been most beautiful. Why should it have changed in its beauty?

Duveen No, you're right. Of course you are. Its beauty has never been an issue.

BB (*turning away from painting*) Thank you for allowing me these moments. They're always precious. It is among his finest achievements.

Duveen Whose?

BB Whose?

Duveen Yes, whose?

BB But surely you know whose? I clarified the attribution a decade ago. At least a decade ago. In fact, I can tell you exactly –

Duveen But as you say, a decade ago, and it was always a slightly uncertain – you yourself were hesitant. You felt that there was more than a possibility –

BB That it is a Giorgione. No, I never wavered in my view that it was Titian. Is a Titian. I considered the possibility that his master contributed a few touches. There are touches that remind one of Giorgione. Here. This fringe – and here, the shading, and – (*Pauses, transfixed in concentration.*)

Duveen Yes?

BB goes on concentrating. Duveen waits, impatient. BB straightens, looks at Duveen.

Well what?

BB Well what what?

Duveen What did you see? What struck you? Something struck you! I saw it strike you!

BB Yes. The exceptional genius of the pupil that is escaping the genius of the master. This is an act of escape, yes . . . Everywhere the influence of Giorgione, and yet – and yet – it is a masterpiece that is completely Titian. A hatching, a moment of sublime hatching. That is what I suddenly – felt. As I'd never felt it before. All the times I'd looked at it. However hard I looked. Never had that moment. Thank you, Joe. It was the last thing I expected this evening. Especially when you have already given me so much.

Duveen You realise now that you are quite alone.

BB Quite alone? Really? In what respect?

Duveen It has been authenticated as a Giorgione by every other expert in the field. But most particularly by Richard Offner. Not even you can deny his authority.

BB Nor his integrity. I'm sorry that we disagree. But there we are. I for Titian, he for Giorgione. An interesting debate. History, I suppose, will decide between us.

Duveen I can't wait for history. I need to know now.

BB Why?

Duveen You know why. The difference between a Giorgione and a Titian is a difference of – of –

BB Plenitude, perhaps? Because there are many Titians, few Giorgiones, but what matters, Joe, is that this is, as you say, a glory, a magnificence in itself, whether painted by the prolific Titian, as it was, or Giorgione – who, I've often thought, by the way, would always have hoarded his genius, releasing it after long intervals of creative contemplation, even if he hadn't died young.

Duveen That's as may be, that's as may be – the fact is he died young, and – and we owe it to him, to our understanding of his genius, to give him the reputation he deserves.

BB But of course.

Duveen By assigning to his name his few and precious works.

BB But because they're so few and precious we must be particularly careful not to be careless – or greedy – in our assignations. Grant one here – (*gesturing to painting*) – merely to increase its market worth, and soon we'll be granting another one, and then another one – why, even in market terms, Joe, that finally becomes bad business, doesn't it? The more Giorgiones, the less valuable each becomes. You were saying as much yourself, of Titian. You would be doing yourself a disservice by persuading me to convert this Titian into a Giorgione.

Duveen It is not a Titian! It is not a Titian! It is a Giorgione!

BB Very well. It is a Giorgione.

Duveen At least accept the possibility –

BB Ah.

Duveen You can do that, at least.

BB I accept the possibility that I might be wrong. I've always accepted that possibility. As I admitted not many minutes ago – as I say fairly frequently – I do not believe in living with my mistakes.

Duveen You are living with a mistake now.

BB I'm perfectly willing to do so as long as I believe it isn't one. Matters like these are matters of opinion. Informed opinion. I acknowledge a mistake when there is further information that alters my opinion. There has been no further information to alter my opinion on this painting and its attribution.

Duveen Not even the knowledge that every other informed opinion is against you?

BB Least of all that. That is not further information, merely further opinion. And I have to back my own opinions, Joe, don't I? Or what would be the use of me? What would have been the use of me to you, in the past? The profitable past? I have been, you might say, your golden opinion.

Duveen You admit you've made mistakes. What's more, BB, what's more, I've known times –

BB (*after a pause*) Joe?

Duveen When you've been in doubt you've gone where the advantage is. (*Little pause.*) The profit. (*Little pause.*) Sometimes when there's been only the slightest, the very slightest, doubt.

BB I hope that that is not true.

Duveen But you admit it might be. Oh, you know I could specify them. (*Little pause.*) I will specify them. For instance the Bellini –

BB I admitted the doubt.

Duveen Yes, but you reversed it. You minimised your doubt, you exaggerated your confidence.

BB The doubt is there. Acknowledged. Published. A published doubt is an alternative conceded. That is what mattered.

Duveen Then admit your doubt in this case. Give Giorgione the benefit of your published doubt. That will be enough. I'll settle for that.

BB You'll settle for that?

Duveen Furthermore, you'll be doing yourself a favour. You will be saving yourself future embarrassment if you admit to the possibility that this is Giorgione.

BB 'Settle for that'? *You* will settle for that? On whose behalf will you settle for that?

Duveen (*after a pause*) Mellon's.

BB Ah.

Duveen This is to be his last acquisition. His last great acquisition.

BB From you?

Duveen Of course from me. He acquires only from me.

BB But he will only acquire his last great acquisition if I am prepared to authenticate it as a Giorgione?

Duveen (*shrugs, nods*) I can persuade him to settle for your not attributing it to Titian.

BB You will interpret the refusal in your own terms?

Duveen When it comes to it, you have only to remain silent.

BB I would have to withdraw my previous attribution to Titian, surely?

Duveen You need do nothing.

BB Ah. (*Little pause.*) I see. You will announce that it is a Giorgione, you will announce the source – the eminent source –

Duveen Sources. Sources. Everyone but you. Everyone that matters but you.

BB And as long as I keep the peace. Publish nothing on the matter. Hold my tongue.

Duveen I would never ask you to do that, BB, hold your tongue, as soon ask a river to hold its flow.

BB You mean I'll prattle away, regardless.

Duveen When the subject comes up, you'll be unable to resist giving your views. I know you. I accept that. It would be pointless not to.

BB Well then – we've come a long way. From begging for my authentication of Giorgione to allowing me freedom to confirm that it is a Titian –

Duveen Privately. Privately you can confirm it as a Titian. Even though you are not a Titian. (*Goes to painting, almost cuddling it.*) You are a Giorgione. On every centimetre of your canvas it is evident, to my eye, Giorgione himself is crying out from the canvas, this is by me, this is me, here I am, at my greatest, why deny me, how can you deny me my being who I am? But you (*to BB*) are at liberty to deny me his being who I am. Privately you can pass me off as Titian.

BB Thank you.

Duveen Just as long as you publish nothing. That is all I ask.

   BB nods.

You agree, then?

BB At the moment I merely acknowledge your proposal. (*Glances at the painting, then as if drawn to it against*

his will, goes to it, studies it.) It is certainly true that
without Giorgione this painting could not exist.

Duveen If you would say that much – just that much
and no more, then I would be satisfied. I could be
satisfied. You would have honoured our contract.

BB (*continues to study the painting*) What contract?

Duveen Our partnership.

BB Ah. Our partnership. Our partnership. Yes. (*still
studying painting*) These faces – the faces of the two
kneeling shepherds – when I try to remember them I can
never see them properly. However hard I try. I have
an impression, of course, a strong one – of intensity,
of devotion, but I have no sense of them, of their
particularity – and now of course I realise why. Because
of course one can't see their faces. (*Laughs almost
childishly.*) Isn't it ridiculous, that one never remembers
that? And yet one should, because that's how it brings
the eye – the whole eye – to Mary, Joseph and the baby –
just as you'd do it on stage, a stage grouping, really, as
elementary as that – crude almost, until the eye goes
beyond, to the boys under the tree, beyond them to the
church, then beyond to the mountains, the clouds – one
has his hair cut *en brosse*, the other longer, almost ill-
kempt, now I've said it I shall remember that much in
future – yes, everywhere present, nowhere visible, like
God, our Giorgione, in this great picture. A spirit and an
influence, you see, Joe, permeating the muscles, sinews
and bones, all of which belonged to Titian. (*turning to
Duveen as he finishes the sentence*) But excuse me, what
were you saying about our contract, our partnership?
You were telling me how I was to honour it, were you
not?

Duveen How you might honour it.

BB Might?

Duveen Well, might in the sense that the contract hasn't yet been drawn up, the partnership – as yet the partnership doesn't exist, BB.

BB And might not exist, unless I honour it, is your meaning, is it, Joe?

Duveen (*after a little pause*) What kind of partnership would it be if the partners contradicted each other?

BB United in purpose, like the Hitler and the Duck? Now there's a partnership that's honoured with every lie, every brutal flouting of laws and agreements, pacts and promises –

Duveen Unworthy! You are being unworthy, BB! The comparison is disgraceful, disgraceful – (*Sits down. He is shaking, upset.*) How dare you, how dare you?

BB Yes, perhaps. Perhaps. (*Little pause.*) Perhaps what I'm trying to say is that our times have become so poisoned that we must cherish the truth, the absolute truth, in all matters in life. We must be on guard against our most acceptable weaknesses – the weaknesses that we're in the habit of accepting with a shrug, an apologetic smile, as for instance, 'Yes, of course I believe it to be a Titian, but on the other hand, out of friendship, out of concern for our partnership, as a way of honouring that partnership in public, and in order to get the contract signed and settled, why not, why not, for God's sake, nod it through? No need to speak even, just a nod that nods it through, a nod in my sleep, even Homer nodded once or twice, now and then, why shouldn't BB nod, just once, now – what difference?' Think of Europe now, think of what awaits it tomorrow, what difference then a little nod in a Tuscan library at midnight, a little nod from BB to Joe . . . ?

Duveen You don't even have to nod. You don't even have to look the other way. I've told you, you can say what you like to whomever you like, as long as you don't say it in print. And you have admitted you can't be sure. You've acknowledged that you might be wrong. Why are you doing this, BB? What do you want that I haven't offered? Speak. Tell me. What do you want?

BB What I want I can no longer have.

Duveen Ask!

BB I want you not to have made our partnership dependent on my acquiescence.

Duveen On your silence only.

BB For me, my silence would have been an acquiescence.

Duveen You mean, it's a matter simply of my having put it into words? (*Laughs.*) You can't mean that?

BB says nothing.

I never spoke them.

BB You spoke them.

Duveen I didn't mean them. You misunderstood.

BB You meant them. I understood.

Duveen And therefore you'll – what will you do?

BB I shall publish to the world my view that *The Adoration of the Shepherds* is a masterpiece of Titian's apprenticeship to his great master, Giorgione.

Duveen That every brush stroke – every stroke of the brush – is Titian's, only Titian's. You could say that, could you?

BB Of course I couldn't. Nor would I. It would sound most eccentric. Mad, even, to account for every dab and daub in any picture ever painted, unless I sat with the artist from the moment he began to the moment he ended. Good God, Joe, I don't claim to be omnipotent, merely an authority, and it is merely as an authority that I shall give my verdict that this is Titian, not Giorgione.

Duveen Which will be enough to prevent Mellon making the purchase.

BB says nothing.

It will go to Kress.

BB Ah.

Duveen To Kress. It will go to Kress.

BB It won't if you don't sell it to him. Keep it until my opinion is forgotten or proved wrong.

Duveen It is not mine not to sell. I am merely an intermediary, trying to get it to Mellon and keep it away from Kress. Kress has become ravenous. (*Little pause.*) He will buy it and exhibit it – God knows where he will exhibit it – (*Laughs.*) – but wherever it will be, it will be an insult. Furthermore, he will exhibit it as a Giorgione.

BB Then you have the ideal purchaser. One who doesn't give a fig for my views. (*Laughs.*) Still, not a negotiation that you care to be associated with, even by default. Certainly not at this stage of your career, eh, Joe, with your trusteeship of the National Gallery? (*Gestures sympathetically.*)

Duveen (*stares at him, as if realising*) You think doing this will be your salvation. Is that it?

BB I suppose that with salvation, too, one is always obliged to start somewhere.

Duveen No, you don't mean salvation, you mean reputation. Well then, it's time somebody told you, BB, you no longer have a reputation. Except in the market place, and with Mellon, alas, a dying man clinging to his sad old habits. But among the tellers of reputations, yours is pretty well known these days for the uses to which it has been put over the years.

BB Ah. A fallen angel, then.

Duveen Perhaps when you were young and beguiling, you might have seemed an angel falling.

BB And now I am an old whore.

Duveen Perhaps shortly too old for the market place, even you will have to skulk here in I Tatti with diminishing funds and when you die Harvard will reject your legacy, your reputation will have tainted it, your collection will be dispersed around the world and I Tatti will become what? An old people's home, a hotel for American or German tourists, depending on the war and its outcome, perhaps there will be a suite or a public room named after you, yes, the Bernard Berenson Lounge, where businessmen can do deals and then take cocktails with their weekend girlfriends. And as for your gardens, the chapel –

> *Looks at BB, stops, giving up, as he realises that BB, oblivious, has gone back to the painting. Duveen goes to painting to take it. BB lets out an involuntary cry.*

Yes?

BB Mmmm?

Duveen I thought you spoke.

BB Leave it a little longer.

Duveen Why?

BB So that I can look at it a little longer.

Duveen Why?

BB Just a few minutes, Joe.

Duveen I would prefer to be on my way.

BB Joe, Joe, you're being petty. That is not you.

Duveen hesitates, replaces the picture.

Thank you. (*Turns away.*)

Duveen And what did you see this time?

BB Only the picture. Nothing else. No names, no dates, no history. Only the picture. Now I have it here, as it should be. Worthless. Beyond worth. Mine.

Duveen I am very happy for you. Can I at least hope for your silence, then?

BB Absolutely not. The moment I hear that it has been ascribed to Giorgione, I shall fire off a contradiction. In fact I shall probably write the contradiction tomorrow morning, first thing when I get up. Finished business, merely requiring posting. When the moment comes.

Duveen And this is not being petty?

BB Ah, but the question is – is it like me?

Duveen You are not a good man, BB.

BB shrugs.

Nor are you an honourable one.

BB shrugs.

But of course you hope you can suddenly convert yourself into a good and honourable man with one last lie.

BB The usual mistake of many civilised men, I should think, when they feel that they're running out of time.

Duveen I've always longed to look into you as you look into paintings. But your eyes are never still. Can't you keep them still?

BB (*coming over to him*) I think I can keep them still when I look into yours.

> *They stare into each other's eyes, BB smiling, Duveen frowning with concentration. BB breaks away.*

Duveen I haven't finished!

BB Yes, you had. I saw what you wanted me to see. How long do you have?

Duveen (*goes to chair, sits down, as if suddenly collapsed. His speech becomes feebler*) Five years ago they said I would last three months. The five years are now up, I believe.

BB I am sorry.

Duveen Thank you.

BB But I can't buy you a further period of life by changing my opinion about the attribution of a painting, can I?

Duveen And if you could, would you?

BB For your life?

Duveen Any life?

BB For the life of someone I loved, almost certainly.

Duveen But certainly not for mine?

BB (*laughs*) Oh Joe, really, you're being disgusting. You'll probably have yellow eyes for another five years. Ten.

Duveen I shall be dead within the three months. You have my word on it.

BB Very well. I accept it, as always, your word. It changes nothing.

Duveen (*after a pause, pathetically*) But if you could save me –

BB Why, then of course you would live, Joe. Just think of that. If I could change Titian into Giorgione I might also be able to turn sickness into health. And you would live. But as I can do neither, Titian will remain Titian, and you will die.

Duveen And if you were to die now, before making your views on my Giorgione public, it would be from that moment forth and for evermore a Giorgione.

BB Are you thinking of murdering me, then, Joe?

Duveen (*laughs, suddenly more robust*) Yes. This evening it would be a great pleasure, BB, to know that I would outlive you.

> *Goes to the painting, takes it to the case, puts it in carefully, is about to close case with a flourish. Before he can do so, Mary enters. She is clearly drunk, but not incapable. She is in her nightie, dressing gown, hair loose, all a bit free-flowing.*

Mary There it is, the laugh, the famous laugh, Nicky said I was dreaming, but I knew I'd heard the bell and that she'd let somebody in – (*going to Duveen, who has deliberately left case lid up*) – and I had a feeling it was you, Joe, dear Joe, come to save us.

Duveen In the flesh! (*wrapping her in his arms*) I'd hoped to get a tiny glimpse, and a hug –

BB My dear, are you sure you should be up, you were feeling a little sickly?

Mary Already better for seeing Joe, but oh, Joe, we don't know where we are any more, with Duck and his Hitler and their hateful politics and threats of war – we can't really be in our Italy, our beloved Italy, can we? We're in some nightmare other country, what are we to do, Joe, what's to become of us?

Duveen I don't know, my dear, these are terrible times, terrible – but then – but then as my old grandfather in Delft used to say, whatever we do the world goes on spinning, each day has its tomorrows, and each tomorrow will have its yesterdays, whether we're on the earth or under it.

Mary (*laughs*) Well, perhaps it sounds more consoling in Dutch.

Duveen No, it sounds more depressing in Dutch, but he said it in Yiddish, if he said it at all – I have only my mother's word – she used to quote it whenever we were fractious –

Mary Oh, yes, yes. (*going to decanter, pouring into glass*) I say much the same to my grandchildren, though I do try not to. 'It'll all be the same in a hundred years,' a thought that would make them cry even louder if they thought about it, poor little darlings – but has he offered you anything, a glass of wine? I can see that he hasn't, really, BB, because he's an old and dear friend doesn't allow you to be a neglectful host –

BB Joe doesn't drink wine, remember, and actually, that isn't wine, my dear, it's brandy.

Mary (*sipping*) My dear?

BB You seem to have poured yourself a glass of brandy, which you've been told not to drink, instead of wine, which as a matter of fact you've also been told not to drink, as both do great harm to your stomach, where most of your problems are.

Mary (*with a laugh*) Oh no, my dear, no, I don't think that's where most of my problems are. But tell me, Joe, my dear, how are yours, Elsie well – and Dolly, any signs of a grandchild?

BB (*cutting in*) Does Nicky know that you're up and running about like this?

Mary I have no idea, but perhaps you should go and find her, tell her to make sure there's a bed made up for Joe in the room he used to have –

BB There's no need, Joe isn't staying the night, he's just leaving.

Mary looks at Duveen.

Duveen Alas, my dear! I have a car, a train, a boat –

Mary But you can't have just popped in for a few minutes after all this time – and you look tired, Joe, tired and – good Heavens, you're incomplete, where's your cigar?

Duveen Ah, the doctors, my dear. Only for celebrations.

Mary Then we must find something for you to celebrate. (*looking at him more closely*) Dear Joe. (*Smiles at him fondly, then serious.*) Something's the matter, what is it? (*Little pause.*) You've been quarrelling again, haven't you, I can feel it in the atmosphere, oh really, I don't, I simply don't understand these – these tumults between you, when everybody knows you're so fond of each other, you have such good times together, jolly times, and yet you always, always have to go through at least nine tumults before you. work things out. Now whatever this is about, come, start again, listen to each other, talk to each other, be kind to me, sweet Joe, darling BB, no more tumulting.

Duveen How can there be tumult, my dear, at least from me, now that you're in the room? Furthermore, furthermore, my dear, I've offered him a full and equal partnership – I can't be kinder than that, my dear, can I?

Mary A full – a full and equal –

BB I have rejected the offer, which was conditional on my changing an opinion I cannot change, and now he is leaving, so there will be no more tumult from me either.

Mary Opinion, opinion about what?

BB It no longer matters –

Duveen simultaneously gestures Mary towards case.

Mary (*goes over to look down*) Oh yes. Oh yes. Of course. Of course. (*Claps her hands joyfully.*) It had to be, hadn't it? (*Takes it out, props it on the lid of the box.*) Well, you haven't forgotten how to pass yourself through customs, have you, Joe?

Duveen No, I was saying to BB – your hat-boxes! Your false bottoms!

Mary Yes, yes, how we could smuggle, the three of us! What fun we had! (*gazing at picture*) Just look at it! The thing itself! The beautiful thing itself! Oh! Oh! That people should quarrel, should ever quarrel, over this. (*in a low voice*) That face. How I love the boy's face! How did he do it! Oh, I wish we could keep it! – well, there, there – (*Puts it reverently back in the box.*) – At least I'll be able to claim that once, for a few minutes, we had Giorgione himself here in I Tatti.

Duveen Giorgione! You believe it to be Giorgione!

Mary We've had arguments now and then. He's wavered, now and then.

BB I am not wavering now. Joe has managed to confirm me in my original opinion. And unfortunately, my dear, it's my opinion he needs, not yours. You should be in bed. Please go. Any further discussion on this will make you ill. I'll get Nicky.

Mary No. No you won't. You'll leave her be. (*Sits down.*) Joe. Here. You come here, please. Sit by me.

Duveen hesitates, goes and sits beside her.

I know how difficult things are for you at the moment, Joe, how hurt you must be about all this fuss at the National Gallery, but Joe, you know, for what it's worth, take it from this old woman, your old friend, it doesn't matter – what you've already given no other man alive could give, you can withdraw now in honour and triumph, to hell with their trusteeship, just another of their bogus English honours, and you've got enough of them, with your knighthood, your lordship, and what have they brought you? Nothing that you can hold, eat, kiss, love, and have they changed the way people who know you feel about you? Of course they haven't, really they just surround you in a fog of unimportant importance for people who don't know you, a photograph in the newspapers they hardly bother to look at, they'd rather look at the face of a cinema star, the wreck of a train crash, any day – the only truth for those who know you and love you is that you're Joe, Joe Duveen, who has done the world some service, indeed he has.

Duveen (*takes her hand, pats it, evidently moved*)) Well, thank you, my dear. Thank you. But with the trusteeship, you know, it's not the honour –

Mary Of course, of course. (*catching his hand*) But now what you must do is rest. Send away the car, spend the night. And then in the morning, when you're both fresh, you can talk again. Have fun. Your usual fun. You've had the quarrel, let the fun begin.

Duveen My dear, I'm afraid that I really must –

Mary (*urgently*) He needs you, Joe. So do I. We all do. Without you we won't be able to pay our bills, there'll be no I Tatti, he'll have no memorial, and there's my family, Joe, you've met my daughters, haven't you, Rachel and Karin? I've told you about their diffculties, now there are the three grandchildren, Rachel's Barbara and Christopher, and Karin's darling Ann, and Rachel's bringing Barbara and Christopher over the week after next, Christopher is such a bright and demanding little boy, and they all rely on me, you see, Karin and her Ann as well, and so really, they all rely on you too, poor Joe, everyone, everyone does, but I'm sure he's too proud to explain our real situation, but I beg you –

BB (*who has become increasingly enraged, snaps the case shut, brings it to Duveen*) May I remind you, Mary, may I remind you, my dear, that here, in I Tatti, the tradition is to dispatch beggars with our best wishes, not to beg from them ourselves. Now listen to this, these are my last words on the matter, regardless of the future of I Tatti, of myself, of my wife, of my wife's children of my wife's grandchildren, of my wife's great-grandchildren, and of my immortal soul. It is my opinion that the Giorgione is a Titian, the Titian is a Giorgione – (*Stops, realising, lets out a barking laugh.*) no, the other way around, no, not that either, let us just say that whichever opinion is the one that is most inconvenient to all concerned is the one that I shall hold fast to until my dying day. If Giorgione himself were to appear before us and claim *The Adoration* as his own, I would be obliged to contradict him. And if Titian were to appear and attribute it to Giorgione, I should do the same. No words could be more final, surely. So now, Joe, if you please. The household needs its rest.

Duveen (*stares at him blankly, stares at Mary, also blankly*) My dear – BB, would you mind if I – I – I feel such a need for – oh yes! (*Gropes desperately in his pocket.*) May I? (*Takes cigar out, unwraps it, lights it, draws deeply.*) Oh. Oh. There we are! And the devil take the hindmost, eh! (*Looks around, smiling, sees case.*) Oh yes. (*Gets up, picks up case, collects his hat.*) Mary – Mary, my dear, you get well, that's what you must do. And BB – no need to see me out, Miss Mariano will open the door for me, I'm sure, with one of her smiles. Such a smile. (*Goes to door.*) The war. There's going to be a war. So leave this country as soon as you can. That's what I've come to say to you. (*Goes out.*)

There is a pause.

Mary (*laughs*) Well, my dear, at least he got what he wanted.

BB Nothing. He got nothing. At least from me. From you he got – (*Gestures in disgust.*)

Mary Oh yes. Whatever he wanted, he got. You never understand with him, you see. Because you do all the dancing, you don't notice that the tunes are all his.

BB pours herself another drink.

BB No. You will not have another.

Tries to take the glass from her. Mary pulls it back. There is a short, unseemly tussle. BB steps away, without glass, the contents of which have been spilt over him.

Mary (*refills her glass, drinks*) How else do you expect me to get through the night, how else, how else? It gives me the strength to endure as I try to understand how it has happened to me, how it is that my life has happened to me, that I am seventy-four and live with my pubescent husband who is seventy-two and his devoted mistress who is fifty-three, and sometimes I'm their charmless old aunt, and sometimes I'm their disgraced infant, but all the time these days I feel like an abandoned mother, BB, I do, I, who did the abandoning – it's come on me so suddenly, like my sickness, it's a craving far stronger than this (*taking a gulp*) – now suddenly when I'm far too old and dying I have nothing to give them. I need to be, need to be mother and grannie day in, day out, as I was meant to be, nature meant me to be, and what do I have instead? (*Looks at him sadly.*) A little old Lithuanian, my only child is a little old Lithuanian child who stole me from my family and put himself in their place, and took me climbing with him into all the dark cellars and lofts, and shone into all the darkest corners and found such treasures in all of them, something that nobody else had even noticed, and remember, remember when you ran through the woods, my little Jewish boy ran into the light, my Lithuanian child, and he stopped, stopped in the light and – stood in wonder – at the miracle – miracle of light, BB – and everything that followed came out that, all of this – (*Gestures helplessly.*) – from my child, my BB, yes, BB mine, my BB – my husband child that didn't come out of me but the woods, the woods – (*Laughs.*) – my BB – my BB – what are we going to do, BB, what, my dear? (*trailing off into a mumble*)

BB What are we going to do – well, my dear, we'll just have to tighten our belts until the war comes, and wipes the slate clean. Think of it, my dear. No history, no past,

no art, no provenance, no debts, no Jews, no I Tatti –
a new age for new men, free men, slate-wipers, clean-
sweepers. So what does it matter, a few lies or a few
truths in the attribution of a Giorgione or a Titian,
one's as good as the other when there's nobody left to
look at them, just the Duck and the Hitler and the new
barbarians, who'll make bonfires of them, along with all
the books – Sophocles, Aeschylus, Plato, Titian, Giorgione,
Leonardo, Edith Wharton –

*Laughs, looks towards Mary, sees that she has passed
out. BB goes to her, looks down at her.*

Come then, come to bed at last, my dear. (*Bends
suddenly, kisses her on the forehead, pushes her hair
back gently, then pulls her up.*)

*Off, the sound of war getting louder, as BB gets Mary
to her feet, struggling to support her.*

Nicky! Nicky! We need you! Come and help us please!
Nicky!

Lights.

SCENE TWO

*I Tatti. Garden. 1960. A summer evening. Nicky, now in
her mid-seventies, is sitting on a bench, asleep. All the
garden furniture different from first scene, very new. On
a small table beside her is a notepad and pencil. Also a
basket, a bottle of wine in a bucket, some glasses. She is
wearing a broad-brimmed hat. Her chin is sunk on her
chest. She is snoring slightly.*
*Over the sound of voices, some coming from the
garden and some from the house, of people chatting,
laughing.*

Fowles enters. Like Nicky, he is now in his mid-seventies. He has a stick, is slightly lame.

Fowles sees Nicky, approaches her, bends down, peers under her hat, as if to identify her.

Nicky lets out a larger snore, like an exclamation.

Fowles straightens, alarmed. Sits down, uncertain what to do. Looks around, sees pad on table, gets up, goes over to it, checks quickly on Nicky, then picks up pad, glances down, starts to read, becomes absorbed, glances at Nicky.

Nicky (*without lifting her head*) What are you doing?

Fowles I'm so sorry, I was – I was just about to leave you a note.

Nicky No, you weren't. You were reading from my pad.

Fowles Yes. Please forgive me. I didn't really mean to, I just – just – I wanted to check on the handwriting, I knew I'd recognise it if you were you. And I did. And you are. (*Laughs slightly.*)

Nicky Well, I'm glad to hear it. Was I snoring?

Fowles No. At any rate, I didn't hear you.

Nicky Sit down, Mr Fowles, why don't you?

Fowles Ah. And you recognise me, then. (*sitting down*)

Nicky It's your tone. Deferential and diplomatic. Old world. Who else could it be?

Fowles I hoped I'd bump into you. Though I didn't really think I'd have the luck –

Nicky I come over quite regularly, to sit here for a while. Especially on afternoons like this.

Fowles Yes, it's beautiful, isn't it? It feels as if nothing's changed. Quite extraordinary. And inside too – every room imbued, yes, that's the word, isn't it, imbued? to the hanging of the smallest painting, the arrangement of the books – imbued with him. And when I remember how worried he was about the money – that Harvard wouldn't be able to afford to take it on –

Nicky Ah well, the war, you know – one of its lessons, that we must preserve and cherish –

Fowles And you don't mind all these intruders – young and American and probably a little brash –

Nicky Fresh. I find them fresh. Not brash. Some of them were BB's students – at least he made them into his students – they gave him such pleasure in his last years –

Fowles And now they're his custodians. How satisfactory it all is.

Nicky looks at him.

Nicky Mr Fowles?

Fowles looks at her.

I'm hearing something in your tone. Too much diplomacy, could it be? Anyway, no longer entirely diplomatic.

Fowles My dear Miss Mariano, I assure you that – nothing could give me more pleasure than finding you here, in such a surrounding and in such circumstances, on such an evening.

Nicky Would you like a glass of wine?

Fowles How kind, but – no, I won't, thank you. But may I pour you one? (*getting up*)

Nicky Thank you. This is my glass. (*holding up glass*)

Fowles Are you expecting company? (*indicating other glasses*)

Nicky I always hope for it. Usually one or two of the students humour me – and you're still on water, are you?

Fowles Yes. Well, no. Actually, if you don't mind – (*Takes whisky flask out of his pocket.*) When I travel. (*Takes a swallow from flask.*)

Nicky Wouldn't you prefer a glass?

Fowles Thank you. But I feel more – more adventurous if I take it direct – as if I'm standing on a mountain top.

Nicky And do you travel much, these days?

Fowles No, scarcely ever. In fact this is my first trip away for – well, years really.

Nicky You've come just to see I Tatti?

Fowles Just for that.

Nicky I thought I might have seen you last April.

Fowles Last April.

Nicky At BB's funeral.

Fowles Oh yes – yes – I thought of coming – but there was a new grandson – and my wife was a bit under the weather – and things at the office – so all in all –

Nicky Have you seen the graves? We've moved Mary in beside him. They're both in the chapel.

Fowles The chapel here?

Nicky Yes. It used to be one of your favourite spots, I seem to recall.

Fowles Yes, yes, indeed it was. Well, I'll – I'll look in on them on my way out. May I ask – are you writing your memoirs?

Nicky I started this afternoon. I think that's what put me to sleep – the effort of remembering forty years – forty years! It might as well be forty days, forty minutes, four hundred years – but, I suppose I've reached the age when I'm always going to be surprised by time, by how little of it has passed, or how much, but none of it continuous. (*Laughs*) At least when I think of writing it down.

Fowles Really? And here I am, at – well, roughly the same age, may I say? – and nothing at all surprises me about time. Continuous is exactly what it seems to be. In that one just gets older. And then older. All perfectly sensible – But forty years – was it really?

Nicky Well, how long were you with Joe?

Fowles Well, from when I was his lift boy, I was thirteen, you know, thirteen. Until his death, when he was seventy.

Nicky I can't work out the arithmetic, from that information.

Fowles Mmm?

Nicky Your having started with him as his office boy at thirteen and your ending with his dying at seventy doesn't tell me how long you were with him, Mr Fowles.

Fowles No, no, of course it doesn't – well, let's see, I was fifty-four when he died, so that's fifty-four minus thirteen equals forty-one or possibly forty, depending on the month of his birth and my death. (*Laughs.*) I mean, of course, my birth and his death. And as I was born in July –

Nicky Let's say forty, Mr Fowles. It rounds us both off so nicely.

Fowles Yes. That's rather a comforting thought – that we both gave the same number of years –

There is a pause.

Nicky BB was so pleased for you when he heard that Joe had left you the company. So was I.

Fowles Thank you.

Nicky And have you enjoyed it?

Fowles I retired last month.

Nicky Really?

Fowles Yes. Just before my board threw me out. They were just about to. On my ear.

Nicky On your ear?

Fowles On my ear.

Nicky But my dear Edward, isn't that the way of the world? Joe's sort of world, anyway. You serve your purposes. And then you get thrown out. On your ear. Really, why not leave it that you retired?

Fowles Oh, I do with the world. And its wife, come to that. Its children too. I'm a retired man, comfortably off, everyone I'm responsible for properly looked after, right down to the great-great-grandchildren, I expect.

Nicky And you have your golf on Sundays. At least I hope you have.

Fowles When the arthritis allows.

Nicky Well then? Why are you angry? You seem to me an angry man, Mr Fowles, but surely you've had a good and useful life?

Fowles (*laughs*) Well, yes – well no, not since Joe's death, since Joe's death I've felt, well – truth to tell, I've felt a bit of a fraud. You see, Joe only left the business to me because in his last months, just after he got back from that visit here, as a matter of fact, he suddenly

became convinced that the people he'd made his heirs –
members of his family, and his lawyer, one of his oldest –
(*Gestures.*) – had been swindling him, and that I was
the only person he could trust, which might have been
true in one sense, but not in another, in that I simply
wasn't cut out to be boss – oh, I suppose I was a decent
enough guardian, I think I can say that much for myself,
at least during the war, but once the war was over, with
all the opportunities – great works of art found under
rubble, or hidden in gardens, cellars, barns all over
Europe, all that loot discovered or recovered, bought,
sold, re-bought – in fact as soon as there were important
decisions to be made, I'd ask myself what would Joe
have done, and then of course I was lost, because the one
thing Joe would never have done is to ask himself what
somebody else would have done – so really the last –
the last fifteen years when it comes to it – I've spent in
a sort of dither, either pretending not to see opportunities
or regretting them when they've gone, really still a lift
boy at heart, you see, needing somebody else – Joe – to
tell him when to go up and when to go down, I sometimes
even found myself wishing that the war hadn't ended –
well, never quite that, of course, how could I, with my
two sons – and the V2s raining down on poor old
London and – and – but – but what a time *you* must
have had in the war, the three of you, still here and in
hiding, and the Germans all over the place – terrible, it
must have been terrible!

Nicky Truth to tell, Mr Fowles – we had a fine time.

Fowles You mean you survived.

Nicky Well, I suppose I mean that BB had a fine time.
Mary of course was here, in I Tatti. Very ill. Dying.
Really, she spent the length of the war dying. But that
was what she wanted. She refused to leave I Tatti. And

as she was a gentile, and very ill, she was safe – I think in her heart she felt she was keeping watch over it for her children. Her grandchildren. It all became a bit muddled in her head. Poor Mary.

Fowles And in what way did you and BB have a fine war? I've always understood that you were in hiding, in fear for your lives. How can that be a fine war?

Nicky You sound angry again, Edward. Do you think we should have joined the resistance – worn berets and darted about in the mountains, shooting the Gestapo?

Fowles No, no, of course not. I didn't mean to sound – just curious. I can't imagine BB cut off from all this – the bustle and glamour of I Tatti, the incessant visits and worshippings – and not minding. Where did you hide then?

Nicky With some friends. They had a little house up in the hills. Very remote. We saw nobody to speak of. We were sometimes frightened. But I've never seen BB so happy. He was liberated, you see.

Fowles Liberated?

Nicky Yes.

Fowles Well, what did he do up there?

Nicky He read. He kept a diary. At certain hours, when it was safe, he walked outdoors and studied and savoured the light. Or sat. But really he did nothing. His only real company was himself. He found out about himself. He used to say that it was Joe that really liberated him. On that last visit – their dreadful row. He felt he'd cleansed himself in some way. After that he felt he could accept anything. The war, the deprivation, the absence of friends – the end of the old life here. Nothing mattered because he was at peace.

Fowles laughs.

Nicky Have I said something funny?

Fowles Yes – I mean, well, the joke of it – that they should both have ended up with what they wanted. Typical of them. And their rows.

Nicky Joe didn't get what he wanted. Quite the opposite, surely. He wanted BB to authenticate the *Adoration* as a Giorgione. BB refused. He was wrong, of course, but he stuck to his guns. So Joe got nothing. And BB got free of Joe.

Fowles Well, the other way of looking at it is that Joe got free of BB, And made BB think it was his decision, which saved a lot of trouble all round. You see, their association had begun to damage Joe's reputation just as much as BB's – he thought the rumours would lose him the trusteeship of the National Gallery. Of course he lost it anyway – but not because of BB. It broke his heart, you know, losing the trusteeship – killed him. Though of course he was dying anyway. But it took a few months off – poor old Joe.

Nicky Poor old Joe. But still, their final row wasn't about money, it was about freedom. And they both won. Let us be glad of that.

Fowles Yes. Although – in fact . . . well, it was also a bit about money. In getting BB to persist in attributing the Giorgione to Titian he . . . liberated BB's attributions. If he could make such a mistake, how many others had he made? All his judgements became suspect. His name lost value.

Nicky I see. So some pictures rose in price, others dropped.

Fowles Well, none dropped, but quite a few rose, is more to the point. Of course, we always honoured BB's attribution when it helped a sale.

Nicky He would have been touched.

Fowles (*laughs*) Not that it mattered for long of course. The war came, and the market changed – everything changed – (*Gestures.*) Tell me, may I ask – you said BB found peace. But what about the end? His death. Was it – was it a – how was it?

Nicky How do you think it should have been? (*Little pause.*) It was as fine as a death can be, for a man of ninety-four. During the last months his mouth was full of ulcers, he couldn't speak. But his smile was quite gentle, his eyes always – spitely, no spright – full of life. BB's kind of life. In the evenings he liked to be carried to the window by his nurses, to watch the light before it began to fade. He saw his last night all the way through to darkness. He died in the morning light.

> *There is a pause.*

(*watching him, concealing amusement*) He received the sacrament before he died. It was administered by the parish priest. He slipped into death an hour later, surrounded by almost everyone close to him. His sister Bessie was there, all the servants, the nurses, Dr Capecchi, his great friend Geromia Giofreddi and his daughter. I was there, of course. So was my sister, Alda. Alda said afterwards that it could have been a scene from Rembrandt. And it was true. His death could have been a scene from Rembrandt.

Fowles So he died a Catholic, did he?

Nicky Oh, no. Of course not. Well, who can say, when it comes to it, what he was at the point of death, except

serene? We could see that, but no, I don't think so – but
I asked him to receive the sacrament as a matter of
courtesy, just as I'd asked Mary to receive it. They both
agreed, silently but distinctly, with a nod of the head.

Fowles A matter of courtesy? To whom – to whom
could such a – a – be a matter of courtesy? To a God he
didn't believe in?

Nicky Courtesy to the household, Mr Fowles. I knew –
he knew – we both knew how offended the servants and
all the local people would be in their feelings – Mary
knew it too. They both wanted to be good guests in
the Italy they loved. Their spiritual home. You're an
Anglican, aren't you? You take your religion seriously,
I remember your saying, so you must surely appreciate
the importance of good manners when the soul leaves
the body?

Fowles (*makes to say something, looks at her*) I believe
you're laughing at me!

Nicky Only because you look so furious.

Fowles Well, it's a bit much – a bit much! (*Suddenly
laughs.*) A serene death and a shrine to the memory of
a man who – who – wasn't particularly meticulous, shall
we say, in his dealings with the world.

Nicky You'd have him in hell, would you, for his
peccadilloes?

Fowles Not in hell, but in the other place – purgatory.
Purgatory for a while.

Nicky Ah. But not for the sake of his soul, for your
temper's sake.

Fowles Well, to satisfy a sense of justice.

Nicky And Joe would have to be there too, wouldn't he? After all he was even less – meticulous, shall we say? – and look at *his* shrines – what are they exactly, how many? Go on. List them, Mr Fowles.

Fowles Well, only – well there are the wings for modern painting and sculpture at the Tate. There's the additional wing to the National Portrait Gallery. And a wing for Venetian art in the National Gallery. And of course the wing of the British Museum for the Elgin marbles – (*Laughs.*) All right, purgatory for Joe, yes, I'd accept that.

Nicky And what about for you and me?

Fowles Yes, I'd accept that too. I'm sure my wife would understand. Oh, by the way – *The Adoration of the Shepherds* – did you know that Kress put it in the window of one of his Five-and-Dime stores – as a Christmas treat for his customers?

Nicky He attributed it to Titian, I trust.

Fowles I'm sure he would have, if *you'd* asked him.

Nicky Oh, I'd have asked for BB's final attribution – 'in part to Giorgione, with Virgin and landscape probably finished by Titian'. After all, he was never a man to stand by his mistakes, was he?

Bells chime off faintly, sound of students' voices, also faint.

Are you going to look into the chapel? It's a lovely time to see it. And the view from there – (*Little pause.*) You don't want to?

Fowles No, I don't think I do. There's that little hill, isn't there? And my leg – ah – (*as students' voices get louder*) – and there are your young custodians, coming this way for their wine – I'm glad we've had a chance for another talk. I used to look forward to them, you know – rather as if they were trysts. (*Takes Nicky's hand.*) You used to call me Edward, I think.

Nicky Used I? I always think of you as Mr Fowles. But Edward is nicer, especially after all this time.

Fowles hesitates, then raises her hand to his lips, picks up his stick, goes off. Nicky looks after him, then, as voices get louder, closer, she looks around with joy and pride, lifts her glass to her lips almost as if in a toast.

Curtain.

JAPES TOO

Characters

Jason
Michael
Anita

Act One

SCENE ONE

Time: mid-1960s.

An afternoon in late June, about four o'clock.

A sitting/dining room. A dining table in middle, table, chairs placed informally around it. A sofa, a couple of armchairs. A television set. Lithographs and sketches and photographs of family groups, not clearly seen, on walls. Books lying about. Also books on shelves. Stage left leads to hall, front door, and stairway up to bedrooms, Jason's study. An arch stage left opens on to kitchen, partly visible. A door upstage opens onto Michael's study.

Michael and Jason are brothers, in their late twenties, Michael a year older than Jason. Jason has a bad leg, a deformity from a childhood accident. He uses a stick, which is not in evidence until he picks it up. They are sitting together on the sofa, watching Wimbledon on television. They have an open bottle of white wine near them, glasses. Also a bottle of liqueur.

Jason You know, one doesn't hate all Americans for winning.

Michael But one hates all Englishmen for losing.

Jason Yes, that's patriotism, I suppose. Some Americans are beautiful. Like Gary Cooper.

Michael Bit past it.

Jason He was always past it. Timeless. A timeless American beauty, Gary Cooper.

Michael Robert Mitchum.

Jason Benjamin Franklin.

Michael Wallace Stevens.

Jason Wally Grout.

Michael Wally Grout!

Jason Australian wicket-keeper.

Michael I know that. But how can an Australian wicket-keeper, a very small Australian wicket-keeper –

Jason He only looked small because he was crouching most of the time.

Michael He was small when he stood up. Between overs. He walked small.

Jason American beauty is a broad church. Is he winning again?

Michael Of course. He's got to win again in order to lose properly. (*Gets up.*)

Jason You know, I'm beginning to think something's got to change around here. We've got to change something. I mean, we're not even on pot, because you're too lazy to go out and get it. Everybody else does nothing on pot, but we manage to do nothing, absolutely nothing, Mychy, on – (*Seizes stick.*) – *en garde*! (*Flourishes it like a sword.*)

> *Michael hesitates, then picks up another stick. They stand with sticks upraised.*

Your challenge!

Michael 'Sunday Morning.' First stanza.

Jason
> Deer walk upon our mountains, and the quail
> Whistle about us their spontaneous cries;

96

Sweet berries ripen in the wilderness;
And, in the isolation of the sky,
At evening, casual flocks of pigeons make
Ambiguous undulations as they sink,
Downward to darkness, on intended wings.

*He launches an attack on Michael. They fence skilfully,
Jason agile in spite of his bad leg. As they do so:*

Michael 'Extended wings.'

Jason Yes.

Michael You said 'intended'. 'Intended wings' –

        . . . casual flocks of pigeons make
    Ambiguous undulations as they sink
    Downward to darkness, on extended wings.

'Downward to darkness, on intended wings' was your
version.

Jason Are you sure?

Michael Yes. (*Slips, drops stick.*)

*Jason stands astride him, stick upraised, as if to run
him through.*

Jason Ah-hah! (*Brings it down, stopping at the last
instant.*) 'Intended wings.'–How depressing. (*Goes to
bottle, pours himself another glass.*)

Michael Yes. (*getting up*) Makes them into suicides,
really, the pigeons.

Jason Not at all, just badly equipped for flying. Like the
rest of us. (*Drains off the whole glass.*)

Michael (*glances at his watch*) Christ, is that the time?
I've got to get to the bottom of the page – (*Goes to
door.*)

Jason Ah! You're expecting old Neets, are you?

Michael What?

Jason That's why you want to finish your page. So you can have the rest of the day with old Neets?

Michael I wish you'd stop referring to her as old Neets. It makes her sound unhygienic.

Jason I got it from you. That's what you call her.

Michael No, I don't. Not any more. I've made a point of calling her Anita.

Jason So you have. As if it were two words. An Eeta. An Eeta. Like a measurement. Don't you move an eeta or I shoot – anyway I thought you'd finished your novel, that chap you sent it to – that agent – Weeble –

Michael Weedon. His name is Weedon.

Jason Weedon. Sorry. Anyway, Weedon, he said he likes it, he wants to take you on, don't you trust him?

Michael At the moment I don't trust anybody, least of all myself. I don't even believe in the title any more.

Jason *Some Fitful Fevers* – it's a good title.

Michael What?

Jason *Some Fitful Fevers*. It's OK.

Michael That's not the title. That was never a title. It was just a way of identifying it, at the beginning. The very beginning. Instead of 'work in progress'.

Jason Well, what's the title now?

Michael *Antelopes in Antibes.*

There is a pause.

Jason Why?

Michael It has a meaning. Do you like her?

Jason Who? Oh. An Eeta. Yes, I do. Yes, she seems very – very – from what I've seen of her.

Michael What worries me is – is that I've started worrying about her. I mean, when I should be working I start thinking, thinking, well, she ought to be bloody here by now, and where is she? And then a sort of worry grows, just a little one, never specific, not about her being run over or assaulted or – meeting somebody else, for God's sakes, least of all that – it's more – a worry over the mystery of her – of who she is. That's what worries me about her absence, her lateness – not where or what or why – but who. Who is she? Perhaps the point is – the real point is – that I'm in love with her. I've never felt like that about any of the others. Have you ever known me feel like that?

Jason You used to get very excited about Ingrid.

Michael Ingrid! But that was just the sex. She was an addiction. A brief addiction.

Jason And a bloody noisy one. You know, there's a funny echo that starts in your bedroom and ends up in mine. Seems to run around in the walls –

Michael You can hear us?

Jason You and Ingrid, she used to honk, or by the time it went around in the walls it was a honk, like an angry goose.

Michael And what do you hear these days?

Jason Not much. It's all right. Perhaps just a tad too much oops-a-daisy.

Michael What? What did you say?

Jason Well – you know, when you go oops-a-daisy, one-two and oops-a-daisy –

Michael Are you – are you suggesting it's obscene or something?

Jason (*rolling a joint, lighting up*) No, no, just a bit – a bit public, that's all. Bit difficult to look at when it's going on in front of one. One of her family's mating rituals, is it? Something they do in Yorkshire, passed on from generation to generation –

Michael It's a game. An affectionate expression of – of a kind of *joie de vivre*. I'm sorry if it offends you.

Jason No, no, it doesn't offend me –

Michael Then why mention it?

Jason Because you were asking –

Michael I wasn't asking anything. I was explaining. Trying to explain my need to have her here, in here, living with me, officially. That's really what I'm trying to do. Take it into account, from your point of view. God, I hate the smell of pot.

Jason Neets – An Eeta doesn't. She smokes it too. Haven't you noticed?

Michael Yes, well – I don't like the smell when she does it, either.

Jason But you haven't said anything to her, have you?

Michael The point is she's not – she hasn't – well, she's still a . . . So of course I haven't said anything. But I might. Soon. That's the point.

Jason You sure you don't want to get married and have done with it?

Michael No.

Jason Well, that's all right then.

Michael What is?

Jason That you're sure you don't want to get married.

Michael No, what I said is that I'm not sure I don't want to get married. I am, in fact, very far from not sure. But you clearly took me to mean the opposite. Which must mean that you're the one that's not sure I should marry her.

Jason It was a misunderstanding – a rather complicated double negative that doesn't come out as a positive – muddled semantics, that's all, Mychy. 'Sure' is one of those words that – that –

Michael Christ, I'm trying to have one of the most serious conversations of my life, the most serious –

Jason But I'm being serious. I'm doing the most serious listening of my life, Mychy. I'm being – being – Look. (*Stubs out joint, drains off glass, puts it away from him.*) You're in a state. You see.

Michael Yes, well. Sorry.

Jason I'm only trying to say –

Michael Yeah, I know. It's just that – you always have such a casual attitude with your own – (*Gestures.*) – things – with women. So I assume you're being rather casual with me. About mine.

Jason I don't feel at all casual about yours. There's a lot at stake. For both of us.

Michael For both of us?

Jason Well, all three of us, come to that. But for you and old – her.

Michael And for you, you're saying.

Jason If you're married, then it's all different. Obviously. Completely different from the present set-up. What about the house, for instance?

Michael The house?

Jason Well, I'd have to move out, wouldn't I?

Michael Would you?

Jason Well, yes, obviously.

Michael But this is a – is a – you're virtually making me choose. It's like some Spanish, Spanish – medieval Spanish poem, epic poem – it's a kind of blackmail. I mean, where would you go? I'd feel guilty. Treacherous.

Jason Why should you? It would be my decision and – and perhaps I need to get away anyway – and there's that job, I've been thinking about it a lot, it's probably still open.

Michael Job, what job?

Jason The British Council job. In New Guinea.

Michael What? Oh, that job! It isn't even in New Guinea. It's in Guyana.

Jason Yes, Guyana, the West Indies. One of the islands. And they play cricket. Test matches, now I come to think of it.

Michael No, they don't. It's the place it always rains, so they're always cancelled, and it's not even an island, it's a tip of somewhere South American and it's hot, steamy, jungly. You'd hate it, Japes.

Jason Are you sure? Still, it's a place to start, it's a university job, that's what matters, and who knows,

I might end up as a professor, Professor Cartts of the South American jungle.

Michael No, you wouldn't, with your – your – (*Gestures.*) – health. You'd end up as plain Mr Cartts – 'Mr Cartts – he dead.' And you know it. And that's what I mean by blackmail. Because you know I'd never let you – never –

Jason And how the fuck – how the fuck – do you think you can stop me? (*Little pause.*) I'm going to go, whether you marry – marry An Eeta or not.

Michael Then I'm fucking well not going to marry her, whether you go or not! So you can fuck off anywhere you want to, Japes, just as long as you fuck off! (*Goes to study, slams door.*)

Jason I thought people like us weren't supposed to end arguments with language – language – (*Gets up. Limps to Michael's door, bellowing.*) – of such fucking – fucking –! (*Stops, limps back, forces himself to settle down with joint. Takes a swig of wine.*)

Complacencies of the peignoir, and late
Coffee and oranges in a sunny chair –

Sound of Michael starting up furious typing.
   Jason looks towards door, makes a gesture of derision, concentrates.

And the green freedom of a cockatoo
Upon a rug mingle to dissipate
The holy hush of ancient sacrifice.
She dreams a little –

There is the sound of the doorbell. Jason looks towards the door, to the sound of Michael's typing, which continues.
   Jason takes his comb out of his pocket, flashes it through his hair, gets up.

There is another ring.
Jason looks towards Michael's study again, as he
goes into hall, offstage.
Sound of door opening.

(*off*) Hi, Neets, come on in.

Anita enters. She is in her early twenties, in a floral
dress, sandals. She carries a basket, large and full.

Anita What did you call me?

Jason Neets.

Anita Neets. Neets. Is that what you and Mychy call
me behind my back? Old Neets, little Neets, little old
Neets . . .

Jason Never. Ever. Anything but our most disturbingly
graceful and necessary Anita. No, Neets just hit me as I
opened the door to you, I wanted to be familiar, you see,
and impertinent, for a change, to show you that we mind
about such things.

Anita What things?

Jason Well, your being very, very late, for one thing
Mychy's been through all the phases, impatience,
irritation, worry, dread – until he finally gave up on you
and went back to work. Where have you been, where
have you been?

Anita (*looks at her watch*) Oh – oh, God, I'm sorry, but
I didn't think there was any rush, I mean we're not going
anywhere particular, are we? And as my train was on
time for once, I thought I was early really, so I took my
time.

Jason Yes, but doing what, is the question? I know,
you've been to the insect house at the zoo studying spiders.

Anita No, I haven't, why would I do that?

Jason Well, why wouldn't you?

Anita Because I hate spiders.

Jason Oh, do you? I love them. For the webs they spin and the songs they sing and – and – well, what have you been doing, then?

Anita I've been up at the church, that little church at the top there, just on the corner of the heath –

Jason Oh, St Mark's, a little charmer, isn't it?

Anita Every time I've passed I want to draw it, and there was a wedding coming out, a fat little bride and a fat little groom, they all seemed fat in fact, even the bridesmaids, and so I watched them until they went off in their cars, and then I sat down and drew it. Well, kind of drew it. Had a first go.

Jason Let's have a look.

Anita No. Absolutely not.

Jason Come on, Neets.

Anita No, I say.

Jason Quite right too. Artists shouldn't parade their half-done stuff and then expect compliments – hey, but what about a drink? I'm on wine.

Anita Lovely.

Jason (*picks up bottle*) It's empty – there's another one in the fridge – (*Turns too sharply, slips slightly back, stumbles into chair.*) Damn! (*Struggles to get up.*)

Anita Oh, I'll get it – (*Puts down basket, goes to kitchen.*)

Jason, getting up, goes to Anita's basket, takes out sketch book, looks through it. Anita returns with bottle and a glass.

What are you doing?

Jason Oh, it's enchanting, Anita. And you've put them in, well, whisped them in, the bride and groom, but they're there, aren't they? Fat little ghosts going to their thin little future, and St Mark's, that's the feel of it all right, you know we nearly buried Mummy and Daddy there –

Anita (*goes to him, takes sketch book from him*) You must never ever do that again.

Jason (*seeing her expression*) No. I'm sorry, Anita. I won't. I promise.

Anita It's as if you sneaked into Mychy's study and looked at what he's writing. (*Hands him bottle and glass.*)

Jason But I do. All the time. And I change things if I don't like them. Rewrite whole sections.

Anita You don't!

Jason No, I don't, but it wouldn't matter if I did, nobody would know the difference, it's all circular, you see, like a lavatory roll that never unrolls to the end, just keeps renewing itself. Probably just as well as it's crap, really. Just crap.

Anita Crap? Is it really?

Jason Delicately thought, finely wrought, maturely paced, ironically poised crap. Well, you've read some of it.

Anita Yes, but I wouldn't know, it's all above my head – but – but poor Mychy – (*looking towards Michael's door*)

Jason (*also looking*) Terrifying, isn't it? And moving too, in its way. But the thing is, Neets, it doesn't matter. Not really. Because he'll be a success, you'll see. He inherited the success gene from Daddy.

Anita And what gene did you inherit, Japes?

Jason I think – I think Mummy's driving gene. Yes. (*pouring into her glass*)

Anita I don't think that's funny. (*taking glass*) He was an architect, wasn't he, your father?

Jason He was indeed. Put up mighty fine buildings for people to live in. Tower blocks they're called. And they're only just beginning to fall down.

Anita And what about your mother? Can I ask?

Jason Yes, you can. She was jolly nice, too, thank you. Exceptionally maternal, in my experience. (*Little pause.*) Also did a lot for charities – especially the disabled – (*Taps his leg.*) It stimulated her interest, you know, my accident, my ghastly accident, she used to say, ghastly, ghastly about everything she disliked, especially the traffic, ghastly, ghastly traffic – so one day there was old Daddy miles over the speed limit and going the wrong way down a one-way street just to avoid the ghastly, ghastly traffic and that's where they ended up, underneath the ghastly, ghastly traffic. Just like Oedipus, when you think about it.

Anita (*laughs*) You're very, very –

Jason What?

Anita Didn't you like them, then?

Jason Who?

Anita Your parents.

Jason Oh they were fine, fine, but the truth is we didn't really need them for anything much. Apart from money, food, shelter and love, and they've left us provided with all that. But what about you and your family up there in old Yorkshire? Tell me about them? Are some of them alive?

Anita Lots and lots of them, and more dead than alive most of them. I don't want to talk about them, thank you. I've decided it's time to stop being a Yorkshire pudding – I'm sick of it.

Jason Oh, you're not a pudding. Quite the reverse –

Anita takes bottle from Jason, pours into her glass.

– whatever the reverse of a pudding is, that's what you are. (*Picks up liqueur bottle, pours some into Anita's glass.*) Here. Gives it a bit of flavour. (*Then pours some into his own glass.*)

Anita Well then – well, I might even get a miniskirt – no, not for me, haven't got the legs for it.

Jason Let's see.

Anita looks at him, then pulls up her dress.

Oh yes, you have. Then again you haven't. Distract attention from your lovely face. Lovely and most loveable face, Mychy calls it.

Anita Does he really?

Jason He thinks you're the most lovely and loveable creature in the world, which is why he's in love with you and loves you. Loves you so.

Anita Why haven't you got anybody?

Jason Ah. (*Lights a joint.*)

Anita No, but really, why haven't you? (*Takes joint, inhales, not very practised.*)

Jason Because of you, of course. It's because of you I keep a chaste bed. A chaste bed.

There is a pause.

Anita Go on, then. A chaste bed you were saying you kept.

Jason Because of you, I said.

Anita Because of me.

Jason Can you purr?

Anita Yes.

Jason Go on then. Purr for me.

Anita Why should I? What have you done to make me purr?

Jason strokes her hair. Anita begins to purr.

Jason (*draws her head onto his chest*) Tell me, what do you want from my big brother?

Anita (*purring*) You know what I want. I want the little brother.

Jason From the first moment I saw you.

Anita From the first moment you saw me.

They stare at each other, then simultaneously they move together, kiss; the kiss becomes overwhelmingly passionate, out of control.
Michael opens door, stands for a second watching, withdraws, closing door quietly.
Anita and Jason draw back, stare at each other, shaken.

Jason Christ!

Anita Christ!

Sound of Bach from Michael's room, very loud. Anita gets up, moves away, sees joint in her fingers, takes a quick drag, hands it to Jason.

It's Vivaldi, isn't it?

Jason No, Bach. Bach.

Anita Are you sure? I know it, and I know Bach, but I don't know Vivaldi.

They sit and listen to the music, catching each other's eye, half-laughing.

Door opens. Michael appears at it, then, as if remembering, goes back into room, turns off music, comes out.

Jason Well, which was it, Bach or Vivaldi?

Michael Oh, I don't know, one of those, I never look when I put it on. How is she?

Jason I don't know, I haven't asked. (*to Anita*) How are you?

Anita Hi.

Michael Sorry, I simply had to get to the end of a bit – that's actually right at the beginning.

Anita Oh, that's all right, we've been sitting here boozing away –

Jason We've had the most delightful – the most delightful – (*Takes her hand, kisses it, bows.*) I thank you for it. And now – (*picking up stick*) – I must return to my – my – onions. (*With a flourish, goes out, slightly unsteadily.*)

Anita Onions. (*Tries a little laugh.*)

Michael Christ! (*fanning the air*) Japes and his joints! (*Sits down beside her, stares at her, smiling.*)

Anita You've been writing then, of course. Of course you have.

Michael I've got myself an agent. A bloke called Weedon. I sent him a draft of *Antelopes in Antibes*. He thought it was OK. Actually more than OK.

Anita Wow! That's – that's wonderful, Mychy, I mean it's very important to have an agent, isn't it?

Michael Yes, it is. (*still staring at her, smiling*)

Anita Well then! (*Gets up.*) Here, here, I've done you a present. (*Goes to basket, takes out sketch book, opens it at St Mark's drawing.*) There. It's for you, if you want it.

Michael It's beautiful. I love it. Where is it?

Anita Oh, just – just up the road. St Mark's.

Michael Ah, I know the one – by your flat. I noticed it the last time I was in York – and who are these, these ghostly figures –

Anita Well, a couple of ghosts really, I suppose, but it's not in York – it's up the road. From here. (*Looks at him, bursts into tears.*) I'm sorry, I'm sorry – I've drunk too much, and a bit of pot and – and I'm being silly, silly –

Michael (*goes to her, takes her hands*) It'll be all right, whatever it is, don't worry – there. There. (*Strokes her cheek, holding her to him.*)

Anita Sorry, sorry –

Michael I know what you need. You need – one – two – don't you?

Anita looks at him, not understanding.

One, two and – and –

Anita Oh! (*Half-laughs.*) One – two –

Jason appears at the door, unseen.

Michael One – two –

Michael *and* **Anita** One, two – and oops-a-daisy!

Anita wraps her legs around Michael.
Lights.

SCENE TWO

Five years later.
Anita is lying rumpled on the sofa. Jason is straightening out his clothes. There are pages of a student's essay scattered about.

Anita Are you all right?

Jason Yes, yes, thanks, Neets. A bit jet-lagged still, I expect. (*Looks at her.*) Sorry.

Anita That's all right. It was great to have you back where you belong.

Jason Mmm? (*picking up pages*)

Anita We always say. You always say.

Jason Are there some over there? Some of these?

Anita picks up pages from sofa, hands them to him.

Thanks.

Anita It isn't, then?

Jason What?

Anita Great to be back – it's been nearly a year this time. Actually, yes, a year.

Jason I know. A difficult year. A long and difficult year.

Anita Because you've missed being here? (*She has been straightening herself out, feeling about beneath her uncomfortably.*)

Jason Well, that too, of course. But everything. The faculty politics, island politics –

Anita All that stuff you were telling Mychy about last night?

Jason Yes, that stuff.

Anita (*fishing out page from under her bottom*) There's this.

Jason Oh. Thanks. There's still a page missing –

Anita Oh. Well, it's not here. (*looking around sofa*) It's very precious then? I mean you seem very worried about it.

Jason Well, it's a student's essay. One of my best students. That's why I wanted to show it to you. As I'd been talking about it. I thought you – you were showing an interest.

Anita Yes, well – I thought you were trying to tell me something.

Jason What sort of something?

Anita Well, not about Wordsworth. I've never even read Wordsworth, to my knowledge.

Jason Well, what else, what sort of something else –?

Anita About her.

Jason Her? Oh, her. Sajit. Yes, well, I suppose I was –
because you were asking, you and Mychy keep asking
why I go on doing it, teaching English in Guyana in
what Mychy calls the educational arsehole of the world –

Anita I've never heard him call it that.

Jason Well, that's how he thinks of it, I know he does –
and you obviously can't see the point either –

Anita Well, for different reasons, probably. Or no,
perhaps the same reason – well, we both wish you were
back here, don't we, obviously? That's all.

Jason Yes, well, I sort of hoped Sajit would explain – this
would explain – why I go on doing it, that's all. I mean,
look, she's bright, and quick and has a feeling for
language, our language –

Anita has begun to roll a joint.

– and the only literature she's got is our literature, an
accidental literature, here's all this poetry, Wordsworth's
– I mean, just think of it – even if you haven't read him
you'd know his – his countryside, his world –

> Three years she grew in sun and shower,
> Then Nature said, 'A lovelier flower
> On earth was never sown;
> This Child I to myself will take;
> She shall be mine, and I will make
> A Lady of my own.

> 'Myself will to my darling be
> Both law and impulse: and with me
> The Girl, in rock and plain,
> In earth and heaven, in glade and bower,
> Shall feel an overseeing power
> To kindle or restrain.

> 'She shall be sportive as the fawn –' (*Stops.*)

– but Sajit, however hard she tries to imagine it, any of it – glades, bowers, fawns, sportive fawns – they're not in her blood, she probably has to look them up in a dictionary. But I can help, you see, that's the point for me. I can help her to imagine.

Anita Are you in love with her?

Jason What! Oh, Neets! She's a student.

Anita Oh, Japes! (*imitating him*) So was I, remember?

Jason Yes, well – you weren't my student.

Anita Wasn't I? Sometimes I feel as if I was. But left half-done. Anyway – anyway, Japes, you're different. Not the way you're usually different when you come back – and it's not just not boozing. It's as if something happened. I mean – are you in love with somebody? Well, you're bound to be some day, but I think I've a right to know, honestly, Japes, don't you?

Jason You'll be the first to know, Neets. I'm not not drinking and doping because of some – some girl – honestly! (*Laughs.*) It was just that it was getting so bad, that's all.

Anita Well, something's happened – something's happened this last year, I know it has.

Jason No, nothing, Neets. Nothing's *happened* to do with – to do with – falling in love, anyway. Though actually something did happen to get me off the booze at last. I don't know if I should tell you this. (*Little pause.*) Well, there was this friend, you see, an American. We did some seminars together and – well, in the evenings, virtually every evening actually, we went down to a rum shop – Angry Annie's – and we got into fights. Well, he did. He's that sort of American. Very political. Thinks anybody who isn't fighting for black independence is a

fascist or a coward, that sort of thing – and he liked to
stir it up at Annie's, you know, pick out the largest black
guy in the room, and go over and sort of cuddle him
and – and insult him at the same time – tell him he ought
to be out there hanging whitey from the lamp posts,
not hanging about with types like him. 'Look at me, the
colour of my skin, what's the matter with you, you a
faggot, a big black cowardly fascist faggot?' That sort
of thing, and mostly they'd just push him away and he'd
pass out – me too, sometimes – pass out – but sometimes
they'd beat him up. Which is what he really wanted,
I suppose. Anyway – anyway, one night he picked out
this really tough, really tough – who just beat him and
beat him until he was down on his knees, his head
hanging, vomiting and blood – and I – I don't know
why, I still don't understand it but anyway I – I – joined
in. I – I beat him, beat him and beat him. Harry, I mean.
My friend. Not the black – in fact the black had to drag
me off him. Off Harry. So – so – Harry went to hospital.
I visited him a couple of times. He had no idea – but he
was gone really – here – (*Touches his head.*) The Dean
sent him home – and I – don't do it any more. Any of it.
I stay in my bungalow and I mark my essays and prepare
my classes and – get on with my novel. Try to keep
myself intact, you see. To be intact and finish my novel.
You see?

Anita (*after a pause*) Mychy says it's very good. When
are you going to let me read it?

Jason Oh well, if you really want to –

Anita (*angrily*) Of course I want to.

Jason Well, he's bringing it back from that agent of his –
Weedon – this afternoon. So if Weedon thinks it's OK,
I'll have the confidence – (*Gestures.*)

Anita Huh! (*little laugh*) A whole year – you've no idea, Japes, how you've conditioned me somehow, so there's not a day when you're not here, when you're not here – (*Holds her breasts.*) – not a day when I don't go into your room and lie on your bed and – and pray that when you are here, soon, please soon, you'll still want me. Were you ever in love with me? Ever?

Jason I've never been in love with anybody else. Never expect to be.

Anita (*after a little pause*) Hah! First you give up dope, then you give up booze, now you give up me, then you'll be in love at last. That's the way it'll go. It must.

Jason But the thing is, Neets –

Anita Go on. Say it.

Jason You know.

Anita Still, I want you to say it.

Jason Well, we can't. Ever again. I meant us not to.

Anita But you couldn't resist me, was that it? Or was it out of kindness? Poor little Neets – old Neets – expecting her – expecting her – why did you come back at all then, why don't you just keep away, getting yourself more and more intact until you're dead to me? That would be the kindness.

Jason But I need to see – to see –

Anita Who? Mychy? Or your daughter? Which?

Jason (*little pause*) All of you. You're my family. All I have for a family, Neets. And I love you. All of you. And that's why – that's really why –

Anita Japes, don't be disgusting. Honest is what you used to be. With your whole heart. Existential.

Jason I am being honest. I need you all.

Anita Well, I don't see why I should need you any more. I think I should try not to do that. And your daughter doesn't need you, does she? She only knows you in bits of time as it is, so you have no idea of what she goes through in her life, of what Mychy and I go through – you know, Japes, you've betrayed me, you said you couldn't, you were too feeble and frail, you couldn't cope – but look at you, look at you, Jason, standing there perfectly *intact* – wishing if only you hadn't had your usual coming-home fuck – you could have taken the two of us with you. You should have – should have –

Jason But how could I have? We don't even know if she's mine.

Anita I know. I know whose she is. And so do you.

Jason No, I don't. And nor do you. Medically speaking, it's quite impossible for either of us to know.

Anita She's yours, Wendy's yours, she's yours. Do you know how hard it is for me with him? (*Long pause.*) Do you know how hard?

Jason But you love him. You said you loved him.

Anita I said what you both wanted to hear.

Jason Then you shouldn't have.

Anita runs at him, slapping at him.

Anita Get out, get out, get out of my house. Get out of my home, get out. Get out!

Jason lurches backwards.
  Sound of front door opening, closing.

Michael (*off*) Hi. Hi.

Sound of front door closing.
     Jason seizes stick, scrambles desperately out of room, as Anita scrambles to sofa, sits down.

Anita Hi, darling. (*Picks joint out of ashtray.*)

Michael (*off, clearly taking off coat, etc.*) It's turned bloody cold, no heating in the taxi – (*Enters, carrying a briefcase.*) Hi, darling. (*Beams at Anita.*) Hi.

Anita Hi. Well, you're looking very full of yourself, where have you been?

Michael Well, with Weedon. Talking about Japes's novel. He thinks it's full of talent. Brimming with talent. A real original. Desperate to take him on.

Anita Well, you said he'd like it, didn't you? Clever old Japes. And how is he – how is he, Weedon?

Michael Oh, he's fine, at least in some senses of the word, no, no, in no sense of the word is Weedon *fine*, ever, he must have put on half a stone in the last few weeks – (*picking up ashtray, taking it to waste-paper basket*). We lunched at the Garrick, by the way, Japes will enjoy that, one of our favourite moments used to be Daddy saying he was off to the Garrick, so proud of himself for being a member, poor old Daddy – Japes does an absolutely brilliant imitation – we must get him to do it for you –

Anita What are you doing?

Michael Emptying the ashtray.

Anita But I haven't finished it.

Michael Oh. (*Looks into ashtray, brings it back, takes out joint, gives it to her.*) Sorry, darling, I wasn't trying to make a point, how could I, when I give interviews about the permissibility of the permissive society – it's just the smell, seems to get into my sinuses these days –

Anita Oh, well, I don't really want it anyway. (*dropping it into ashtray*)

Michael No, no, honestly, darling –

Anita Please dump it! (*checking irritation*) I've got to pick up Wendy in a minute, so I shouldn't.

Michael Oh, then we'll put it over here, you can finish it when you get back.

Anita Thank you.

There is a pause. Michael looks at her.

Michael Darling, what is it? What's the matter? What's happened?

Anita Nothing, nothing's happened, it's just – Wendy, worrying about Wendy, I've been worrying and worrying about her. All day. Every minute of the day.

Michael Has there been more trouble, then? Something at school?

Anita No, no, it's just her! Well, you know yourself, Mychy, perfectly well, she doesn't get on wih people, her own peer group, or with us – she's always miserable and sullen and ill-tempered, Michael, she is, and tantrums the moment she doesn't get her own way – nobody likes her, nobody likes our Wendy, Mychy, nobody.

Michael Now that isn't strictly true, darling, look at – look at – Japes. Absolutely fallen in love with he. When he put her to bed the other night he had her yelping with laughter with his 'Here comes the bogeyman', and he actually got her to sing, all quite gooey really, but there's a real bond there – it's not just that he's brought something out in her, she's brought something out in him.

Anita Yes, well, he only does it a couple of times a year, when he bothers to come back, let him try doing it every night, then we'd see how gooey – gooey –

Michael Well, she's not really Japes's responsibility, in that sense, is she? I only mentioned him because you said that nobody – and anyway she's only four, for God's sake, she's not a hardened war criminal, just a – a perfectly normal, normal difficult child. You know the real problem, the real problem is that we're not allowed to accept old-fashioned normal difficult children – nowadays every infant has to conform to some rule of growth – a touch of colic, a few teething problems, some mandatory hiccups in the toilet training. Well, it didn't work like that in our daughter's case, did it? Every aspect of her growth so far – from getting her wires crossed at the nappy stage to gum-boils and thrush and – but then she didn't just – just pop out of you, did she, in spite of all those natural birth classes we had to sit through – she didn't get classes in the womb, there she was, perfectly innocently upside down or the wrong way around and suddenly she was being jerked out by forceps and clamps. Put any creature, especially a new one, in a bad temper, so that's all it comes from really, this famous bad temper of hers, her beginnings, and all we have to do, darling, really, is to be patient until she recovers it. Her temper. Or discovers it. And then her behaviour will be – well, merely as bad as everybody else's. (*Little pause.*) And in the meanwhile we can look at some other nursery schools if you want.

Anita No, Mychy, no, the truth is – we should keep her at home. Yes. That's the proper thing, you know it is.

Michael At home! But darling, I work here – and you – now you've really started on your children's book again – the bedbugs, *Basil the Bashful* –

Anita Boris. It's Boris.

Michael Boris. I couldn't bear it if you had to give up on him again.

Anita We could get an au pair.

Michael An au pair! But we haven't got room for an au pair! Where would we put her?

Anita In Japes's room. Well, it's just sitting there wasted for most of the year –

Michael But darling, it's his. His room. Whether he's in it or not. He still keeps a good part of his life in it.

Anita We could shift all that down to the basement. And when he does decide to turn up, he can doss down in here.

Michael In here. (*Looks around.*) Japes. Doss down in – (*Laughs.*) Legally half of every room in the house belongs to him, have you forgotten?

Anita We could buy him out.

Michael No, I couldn't. He'd never sell. And I wouldn't want to buy – buy him – he was born here. I was here when he was born here. It'll always be here for him, wherever he is.

Anita Just like you, you mean?

Michael What?

Anita You'll always be here for him, wherever he is, which is why he hasn't gone anywhere, really, not even to Guyana, not in his – his soul. He's even trying to turn himself into you, not just – just cleaning himself up but becoming a writer and – and even trying to muscle in on Weedon. He's busy sort of – sort of taking over from you, being you –

Michael What!

Anita Yes. You but without any of the responsibilities of – of a proper grown-up. And you let – no, you encourage him, the heart of him, the soul of him, because he's your little brother and you can't bear to see him get free of you. Your little Japes. Belongs to you. Big Mychy and his little Japes. Well, I want him out, I want that room for my daughter. My daughter's au pair.

Michael I thought – I thought you loved him.

Anita Love him, love him, what's that got to do with it? It's not my love that won't let him move out, it's yours, and all the guilt, the guilt shit you mix up in it, the way you go on blaming yourself is a kind of conceit, anything that happens to him good or bad, it always goes back to you and what you did to him, so really you end up as a sort of God and he's just your playmate. Thing. Plaything.

Michael This isn't you, this isn't Neets, my Neets. It isn't, Neets. It isn't you.

Anita You didn't cripple him on purpose, you were just boys, horsing about in a swimming pool, bouncing each other on a diving board, nothing glamorous or dark or hidden in it, just a simple bloody accident, however you tell it after we fuck, your voice droning on and on with the damage you've done to him. 'Oh woe is me, woe is me that I could mangle mine own brother,' while all the time your daughter, who's in need, real need of your love and care and attention, is denied – denied – (*Turns away, as if ashamed.*)

Michael What? Oh, Neets – my dearest old Neets – (*Goes to her.*) Please, my darling, you can't believe, mustn't believe, ever, that I've made some choice between – between Japes and our Wendy – or you and – and . . . I love you all. To the very best of my – my – I do. And he is breaking free, you know, Japes – his whole thing over there in Guyana, his struggle to become healthy and strong, his taking his job seriously, his writing – that's all part of his trying to make a new life for himself. With the woman he loves.

Anita Loves? Woman he loves?

Michael One of his students, inevitably. She's called Rabbit, no, of course she isn't, Sab – Rab something like that. Anyway the point is that he absolutely adores her, they're head over heels, the two of them.

Jason enters.
Michael breaks away.

Jason Ah, you're back then, I thought I heard your voice.

Michael Yes, I was just coming to look for you, things to tell you, but I was just filling Neets in on the Garrick Club. Remember Daddy in his Garrick Club days, that's where he took me – Weedon.

Anita Yes, do your face.

Jason My face?

Michael That face you used to do that Daddy used to do whenever he was going off to the committee –

Jason Oh. Oh, yes, that one – 'Oh, Debs darling, boys, quite forgotten that bloody Garrick pow-wow –'

Michael (*laughs, looks towards Anita*) Pow-wow, I'd forgotten pow-wow – only time he ever used the word. Anyway, I was just telling Neets, Weedon made me wear a tie he'd brought along especially, wants to put me up for it, he thinks it's a good career move, I suppose, there are editors, possibly even a few literary editors, but just

the thought of Daddy, and your smirking his smirk –
better off, creatively anyway, on the outside, looking in.

Jason Oh, but you're already on the inside, Mychy, at
least as most of the reviewers see it.

Michael Well then, on the inside looking in. (*Laughs.*)
Oh, and look – the fact is, I've been rather indiscreet
with Neets, given the game away. About you and the
lady in Guyana. Your Samji – it is Samji, isn't it Japes,
her name?

Jason No, Sajit. It's Sajit.

Anita Sajit.

Michael Anyway, I just found myself blabbing it out.
Sorry, Japes.

Anita It would have been nicer to have heard from your
own lips, Japes.

Jason Yes, but well actually, it's not really that – that big
a – at the moment it's still a friendship, really. Platonic.

Michael Platonic! It didn't sound at all platonic from
your descriptions – steamy and jungly was the impression
you gave me, one sexy lady. Not that she isn't brilliant
with it, of course, she's got a real intelligence, Neets,
marvellously simple and individual. Have you shown
Neets her essay?

Jason No.

Michael You must read it, darling!

Anita Yes, well, first there's a little matter of our daughter,
our daughter, darling.

Michael What?

Anita It's time for me to collect her, I must dash or I'll
be late again.

Michael Oh God, yes – (*looking at his watch. Goes to her.*) See. Everything's all right. Everything's going to be fine. (*Puts his arms around her.*) In fact it's all going to be – one, two – one, two, and oops-a-daisy, one, two – (*hoisting her up*)

Anita (*her legs clamped around him*) And oops-a-daisy, one, two and oops-a-daisy – (*staring almost crazily at Jason, laughing*)

Michael What's this – you've got something – (*Hands go under skirt.*) Here, got it!

    As Anita unwraps herself Michael is holding sheet of essay.

What is it? (*Glances down at sheet.*)

Anita (*looks at sheet, looks at Jason*) I've got to dash! (*Lets out a scream of something like laughter, dashes out.*)

Michael Oh, darling – take a coat. It's turned cold again.

Anita Right. (*Goes out without coat.*)

Michael (*bellowing*) Neets, a coat!

    Sound of door shutting. Michael looks at essay.

I seem to recognise the handwriting. It's your lady's, isn't it? Her essay on Wordsworth. Yes, here's the quote. (*Glances down at sheet.*)

    Strange fits of passion I have known:
    And I will dare to tell,
    But in the lover's ear alone,
    What once to me befell –

Jason He really is tops, isn't he, old Bill? Billy Wordsworth.

Michael (*nods, continues reciting, not reading*)
When she I loved looked every day
Fresh as a rose in June,
I to her cottage made my way –

Jason Bent. Bent my way.

Michael Yes, of course. Bent my way.

Jason 'Beneath the evening moon' –

Michael 'Beneath the evening moon'. (*Looks at Jason.*)

Jason Well, thank God it turned up before I missed it, I get extremely neurotic about losing students' essays – it must have slipped onto the sofa while I was showing it to Neets. (*holding out his hand for essay*)

Michael But you haven't shown it to Neets yet, you said, didn't you say? Or she say? Or both say?

Jason Ah, well when I was showing it to you, then.

Michael Ah, yes. Except it was in my study – you showed it to me in my study, didn't you? Well, anyway, better not tell your Samji that she ended up on the bum of your sister-in-law, however she got there, or she'll think – God knows what she'll think, eh? (*handing him essay back*)

Jason Probably that we stint on the lavatory paper – eh? (*Lets out a kind of laugh.*)

Michael (*smiles*) Well.

Jason Well – (*Sees his manuscript.*) Well, how did it go?

Michael Mmmm?

Jason With Weedon. My novel.

Michael Oh. Oh, yes. *Torching the Dove.* (*picking the manuscript up*) Not too well, actually, I'm afraid, Japes. He doesn't want to take you on, you see.

Jason Ah. Thinks it stinks, does he?

Michael Not stinks, Japes, nothing you do could ever stink, for God's sake. No, he thinks you've got a talent, write beautifully, lots of good jokes about bad sex – 'lovely squalid stuff' were his words. And he admired – oh, lots of things. Everything except, well, except your tone, really.

Jason My tone.

Michael Apparently it's identical to mine. My tone.

Jason Your tone. And you, what do you think?

Michael Well, impossible for me to say, really, isn't it? I mean, if it is my tone, then I'd be too familiar with it – I'd be the last to know, so to speak, wouldn't I?

Jason I can't imagine any tone less like yours than mine.

Michael Exactly. And I can't imagine any tone less like mine than yours. So it obviously cuts both ways. Our over-familiarity. Of course it's not a matter of imitation, the tone, but genetic – neither of us can help having that particular – tone gene. He thinks a lot of publishers would probably feel the same, that one of me is more than enough. Bloody awful being the younger brother sometimes, eh, Japes? Always the second comer, the second served. Neets was just saying as much a moment ago.

Jason Oh, she was, was she? Mychy, I think I'll go tomorrow.

Michael Oh. Not because of Weedon, I hope.

Jason No, not because of Weedon. It's just that I rather find myself missing the educational arsehole. And the jungly smells.

Michael Well then – oddly enough, Neets was just saying that we should start thinking of an au pair, except there wasn't a room. (*Laughs.*)

Jason Well, there is now. If you could see to packing up my things and shipping them – the bungalow needs them.

Michael And Samji does too, I expect. If she's to make a home with you.

Jason It's Sajit, Mychy. Sajit. And I never let her anywhere near the bungalow. To tell you the truth, Mychy, she's just another of my fucks, really.

Michael Really?

Jason I've been in the habit of saving myself, my best self, for when I came home. You see.

Michael Ah. Well then. Perhaps under the circumstances you'd like to sell out. Your half of the house, that is.

Jason Oh, I'd never want to do that. Too many important things have happened here. It means far too much to me to let go of it. Ever. (*Turns, goes out of the room.*)

SCENE THREE

Seven years later.
    Lights up on Michael on telephone.

Michael (*on telephone*) – oh, of course, sorry, fancy dress, I'd forgotten, they're all in fancy dress – well, she's

there as a wolf – no, no, it's a fox, no, a wolf, I think –
she's either there as a fox or a wolf, a girl too tall for
her age with freckles as a fox or a wolf – and come to
think of it, she may be in one of the corners lying down.
Is any of the girls there prostrate anywhere, on the
floor? Pass me over to whom? Oh, Miss Stokehurst –
(*attempting calm*) – you're one of the teachers, are you?,
Good – well, Miss Stokehurst, the point is we've lost
Wendy – or rather you've lost Wendy – er – anyway,
she's vanished from the party, the point is, you see –
what? No, let me explain, let me explain – my wife is
there somewhere with Mrs – your assistant headmistress –
touring the building looking for – you see, the point is
she phoned us, Wendy did, about half an hour ago,
phoned us at home to say she wasn't feeling well, that
she – she, well, as far as we could make out, some girl,
some imbecile of a girl had given her pills – (*Little pause.*)
Yes, pills, red pills, that she'd somehow got hold of from
her mother, presumably from her mother's bathroom or
medicine cabinet or – or – anyway, she gave some to
Wendy, who swallowed them – yes, yes, that's right,
that's the whole point, that's what I'm trying to tell you –
she swallowed these bloody pills and then when she
began to feel faint she phoned us and told us what she'd
done and I told her to wait there, there and by the
telephone, to try not to sit down or close her eyes, but
when we got there she wasn't there so I've come back
here in case she'd come here but my wife stayed there in
case she was still there and she doesn't appear to be
either – or – so she – I suppose she set off from the
school on her own – at this hour and dressed like a fox
or a wolf and . . . Yes, I know, very cold, very cold, and
if she's coming across the heath – I mean, my God,
across the heath in the dark in the cold, feeling faint and
dressed like a wolf or a . . . The police, yes, perhaps we'd
better – you'd better – look, Mrs – Mrs – where are you,

where have you gone, where the hell have you gone?
(*shouting*) Oh, darling, it's you, where have you been,
where the hell have you been, she's not here, Wendy isn't
here – what? A joke! Not pills, well, what the hell were
they? What, smarties! Well – well, where was she then?
Hiding in the lavatory, right, right – well, well, there you
are, the two of you – are you all right? Well, the thing is,
darling, to calm down – anyway, until you get home –
no, no, I don't think you should come now, we don't
want to make a meal of it, she gets into enough – I mean,
her reputation – much better to treat it all as – as, well,
as a joke. Which is after all what it was. So – so, hang
on, darling – yes, I know, I know, hang on another hour
and I'll come and pick you up – yes, in an hour, on the
dot, I promise – OK, then, OK – oh, and give her a kiss
from me. (*Puts phone down.*) Stupid child, stupid bloody
child – oh! (*Takes off his overcoat, goes over to drinks
table, pours himself a carefully measured drink, goes
upstairs to study.*)

> *Sound of typing.*
> *The door opens.*
> *Jason enters. He is dressed in tropical gear, carrying
> a bag. He is unshaven, almost bearded. He has his
> stick. He puts down bag, clutches himself, shivering,
> casts a glance towards the drinks table, goes to it,
> picks up a bottle of Scotch, takes a terrific gulp. His
> hands are shaking. Becomes aware of the music from
> Michael's room.*
> *Music stops. Typing stops.*
> *Jason takes another quick gulp, puts bottle down.
> Moves away from the table, waits.*
> *Michael enters.*

Michael (*after a shocked pause*) Japes?

Jason Yup.

Michael Well then – Christ. (*little laugh*) Then you're back.

Jason Yup.

Michael You know, I thought – I had a sudden sense that you were here, down here. I knew it. Well, let's look at you properly.

Turns light on, goes to him, stops as if in shock at his condition, then makes to embrace him. Jason averts himself.

Well – hi.

Jason Hi.

Michael You're straight off the plane, are you? You must be – you must be . . . What can I get you? A drink, of course, what would you like?

Jason Oh – have you any rum? (*Goes to sit down.*)

Michael No, sorry – almost anything else. Scotch, cognac, gin, vodka –

Jason Whatever, Scotch, I think. Yes. Scotch.

Michael Well, what does one say? A surprise, I mean – what a surprise.

Jason To me too. I would have phoned, but things were a bit rushed over there, and the lines are always so bad – and at the airport – I didn't understand the coins, I'd forgotten how they worked in the – the – (*Puts his arms around himself.*) – slots. Telephone slots.

Michael (*bringing him drink*) You're cold –

Jason Yes, I'd forgotten that, too – thank you – (*taking drink*) Ice. Like ice. Thank you.

Michael Shall I get you a blanket?

Jason No, I'll be fine. More a matter of internal adjustment. (*Takes a controlled gulp.*) That's better. Soon get the heat – nothing on the plane, you see.

Michael Nothing?

Jason Nothing.

Michael You mean you haven't eaten – all the way from Guyana here – you must be famished, let's go to the kitchen.

Jason Oh, there was food. Food and water. And the usual rubbish. But nothing like this. No rum. Condition of travel, you see. For me anyway. All alcohol forbidden. (*Laughs.*) They filled me with pills instead. And an injection.

Michael Well, is it safe yet?

Jason (*who drinks and refills steadily from now on*) Mmm?

Michael Should you be having one now? A drink.

Jason Oh, yes. Well, I must be because I am, aren't I? (*Lifts his glass to Michael, laughs.*) Mychy!

Michael What sort of pills? Injection? What for?

Jason Mmmm.

Michael Are you ill, then?

Jason Ill?

Michael If they gave you pills and an injection –

Jason Ah. To stop me wanting a drink. Didn't work though. God, I gave them a bad time. (*Laughs.*) Shouted abuse, claimed my rights, made threats – that sort of thing. Very unattractive. But that didn't work either. Had me sort of wedged in my seat so I couldn't get up to do

133

a proper job. Also woozy. No balance. I fell asleep just before we landed. Because of the pills. They got me out of the airport into the taxi, must have because that's where I woke up. In the taxi. Told him to come here. Couldn't think of anywhere else, Mychy.

Michael There isn't anywhere else, Japes. (*Little pause.*) So it's that bad, is it?

Jason Oh yes, Mychy. That bad. (*Nods.*)

Michael And is that the whole trouble?

Jason Mmm?

Michael Your stomach. It's – (*Gestures.*)

Jason Oh, that's nothing. Nothing. Don't worry about that. (*slapping stomach, which is very bloated*) Just liquid. That's why it's tight. Drum-tight. Not flabby. Firm. Drum-firm. Hear it?

Michael Yes. So you're OK otherwise. Otherwise OK?

Jason Otherwise. (*Does a thumbs-up.*)

Michael That's a relief. That you're not back here for your health. Are you still shivering?

Jason Shaking. Not shivering. Mychy?

Michael Yes.

Jason Do you mind if I – (*Gets up, goes unsteadily to table.*) – help myself – (*taking bottle*)

Michael No, no. Of course –

Jason I'm used to having control, you see. Over my own bottle. I get worried (*sitting down*) if I have to depend on other people. I've come to hate dependence. Need to cope for myself. In the university bar I have my own bottle. They used to put my name on it. Now they don't bother. And at Angry Annie's too.

Michael Angry Annie's?

Jason Brute of a woman. Vile temper. Got six children. Says two of them are mine. Don't think so, somehow. Somehow don't think so. Wrong colour. Though you never know, do you, whose child is whose, by what evidence. How is she?

Michael (*after a little pause*) How is who?

Jason Our girl of course.

Michael Ah. She's at a school party. It's a fancy dress. She's gone as a wolf.

Jason A wolf!

Michael Yes.

Jason Neets as a wolf! Grrrr! What a thought! Little Red Riding Wolf, eh, is that it? I can see that. Yes. Quite clearly. Little Red Neets, gone as a wolf.

Michael Wendy. It's Wendy that's gone as the wolf.

Jason Wendy! Oh yes, of course, our daughter. Quite the terror, isn't she? Quite the terror.

Michael Perhaps when you last saw her. I seem to remember she was going through an odd little phase – but she was only three. She's eleven now.

Jason Four.

Michael She's eleven, Japes.

Jason She wasn't eleven, she wasn't three, she was four when I last saw her, Mychy. That Christmas. When we had that little what's-it over Neets. Almost fisticuffs. (*Laughs, wags his fists.*)

Michael Over Neets? No, we never had a what's-it over Neets, Japes. Though there was a disagreement over Weedon, I seem to recall.

Jason She used to write to me a lot. Sometimes several times a week.

Michael Did she?

Jason You knew that, didn't you?

Michael Well, that she wrote, yes, of course I did.

Jason Some of them were a bit mad, frankly, Mychy.

Michael Were they? Well, that's very much in the past, she's working very hard on her book, her children's book, her bedbugs. The illustrations are going to be enchanting.

Jason One, two – oops-a-daisy – one, two – oops-a-daisy, eh, Mychy? (*Laughs lewdly.*)

Michael How's the cold?

Jason Still here. (*Taps chest.*) Can't get to it.

Michael I think – I think you're in a bad way, Japes. Aren't you?

Jason What happened to the dog?

Michael Dog? Oh, wolf, you're thinking of Wendy –

Jason No, Sandy. I'm thinking of Sandy. A labrador. Yours and mine, Mychy.

Michael Oh yes, Sandy. We had him put down – Daddy did – he had distemper.

Jason That's it, that's right, running around in circles, foaming, we thought it was funny, didn't we, Mychy, until Mummy started screaming. Wasn't rabid, though, like me.

Michael Rabid? Japes, you're not – you haven't been bitten – bitten by a dog in Guyana?

Jason stares back at him.

Christ, Japes, well, what have they done, have they given you those shots – is that the injection?

Jason What?

Michael You said you'd been bitten by a rabid dog.

Jason Yes, yes, the Dean – rabid Dean – and the rest of them, the whole pack of them, whole pack of rabids coming at me – grrr! Grrr! (*roaring, yelping, slobbering*)

Michael Oh – oh, I see. A figure of speech. (*Gives a little laugh.*) Well, what were they coming after you for?

Jason picks up bottle, cradles it in his lap, closes his eyes. Michael looks at him.

Oh, Christ, Japes. (*to himself*) Japes, do you know where you are? Japes. (*Goes to him, touches him on the shoulder.*) Japes. I think you need help. Or anyway to lie down, Japes. Old Japes.

Jason (*takes his hand, holds it*) Sweet Mychy. You're very sweet. (*Kisses Michael's hand.*) There. I'll be all right. I need to talk to you. Sit down, you're looming again, just the way I always think of you. Go on, Mychy, sit. Please. (*suddenly roaring*) Sit, I said!

Michael sits.

Thank you.

Michael Can you tell me what happened?

Jason Mmm?

Michael Well, why you're here suddenly. It's the middle of the term, isn't it? (*Little pause.*) Why did they come after you? What did you do, Japes?

Jason Christ, Mychy, those reviews you get – I see all of them, always, in the common room, they come late of course, still reading one batch of reviews and there's another novel plopping out, and then while I'm on the reviews of that out plops another novel, and another and another, plop, plop, plop – Christ, I'm proud of you, Mychy, boast about you all over Guyana, made you big in Guyana, what was it you've got, Daddy got too, a CBO, is it?

Michael An OBE.

Jason And perhaps a knighthood like Daddy, Sir Mychy Cartts – Sir Mychy and Lady Neets Cartts, do you think she'd like that? I would. Wouldn't mind being Lady Neets Cartts myself – (*Laughs. Begins to choke slightly, gets himself together.*) Sorry, Mychy. Sorry. (*Little pause.*) Gets like that, you see. At a certain point. It's the blood. Bad blood. Black. That's why they've sent me to you. Because of the bad, black blood. That's what they say. But it's not the real reason. The real reason is politics. Politics and women. Americans. Three of them. Doing a tour. A tour of Caribbean us. Us.

Michael Universities?

Jason Us. Us. Us! (*slapping his chest*) In the common room. My common room. On their arses. With their grants. Their doctorates. Their publications. Their – their – feminist – feminist – one of them in my chair. Everybody knew it was my chair. My bum shaped it, term in, term out, gave the cushion its – its – depth, its meaning, its value, my bum did. My bum. That's the point, Mychy, it was my bum, my chair.

Michael I see. And so you were offensive, was that it?

Jason Polite. I was extremely polite, Herman. (*Nods, falls silent.*)

138

Michael Herman?

Jason Herman?

Michael You called me Herman.

Jason Oh. No, he's dead. One of the friendly dead. Australian geologist. I'll probably visit him in Sydney.

Michael Please, Japes, you should lie down.

Jason Why?

Michael Because you're drunk, Japes. Exhausted. And I don't want Anita and Wendy – Wendy in particular – you wouldn't want her to, either.

Jason Sitting on their arses in my chair in my common – 'What would you three ladies like to drink?' 'Don't call us ladies,' very offensive to be called ladies, and I said, 'What then, what do I call you?' and they said, 'Anything, anything but ladies,' so I said, 'Right then, right, what can I get you three cunts?' (*Begins to laugh.*) Cunts, I called them – cunts – 'What would you three cunts –' and then I took it out – (*Stands up, swaying, unzips his flies, gropes for his penis.*) 'Here, cunts, have a look at this, have a look at this!'

Michael Yes, Japes, all right. (*putting his hand preventively on Jason's arm*) I get the – the –

Jason I keep my pension though.

Michael Japes – Japes – come along, Japes, come along. (*attempting to take Jason's arm*)

Jason (*pulling violently away*) You listen to me, Mychy, you listen to me. This is my house, half of this is my house, you can't throw me out of it, Mychy, you can't keep me away from it – I own half and I want it. I've come back for it. I'm taking it and I'm taking my half of everything else, Mychy. My half of our daughter, my half of the wife, the half that belongs to me. Do you understand, Mychy? Understand it?

Michael Yes, of course, Japes. You'll have everything that belongs to you. Of course you will.

Jason Just half, Mychy, just my half. No more, no less, just my half.

Michael Yes – yes, just your half. Now will you come with me and lie down? Just for a while. Just for a little while. When you wake up, there'll be Neets and there'll be Wendy, and I'll be there. And you'll be in your family again.

Jason My family again. Oh, Mychy, my family again – oh, Mychy – oh, Mychy – (*Holds his arms out, lurching.*)

> As Michael goes to him, Jason reels away and collapses to the floor.
> He is making retching sounds, goes still as death, face turned up.
> Michael goes to him, takes him in his arms, cradles him.

Michael Oh, Japes, my Japes – (*Lets out an animal howl of grief.*)

> Lights.
> Curtain.

Act Two

SCENE ONE

Five years later.

There is a student's briefcase on the floor, contents, including purse and keys, scattered about. Also some papers, books. A transistor radio is lying on the floor, playing popular music, loudly. The television is on.

Anita is sprawled on the sofa, drinking a glass of wine. She has a bottle beside her. Also a drawing pad, a case of pencils, etc.

There is a ring at the doorbell.

Anita registers it, looks towards door. Front door opens, off.

Jason enters. He is carrying a carrier bag. He uses a different, up-to-date, stick, walks more easily.

Jason Hi. (*then raising his voice*) Hi!

Anita Hi!

Jason May I make some silence?

Anita What?

Jason Turn things off.

Anita Oh, yes, yes. I'd almost stopped noticing.

Jason turns off television set, goes to turn off transistor.

Jason (*fiddling with transistor*) I don't know how you do these bloody –

Anita Oh, just smash it to death is what I long to do – but this is what I usually do. (*Puts bottle down, takes it, opens the back, shakes out batteries.*) Hi, Japes.

141

Jason Hi, Neets.

Anita Thanks for coming round.

Jason Well, you sounded – you sounded desperate on the phone.

Anita Sorry, I was in a state. Actually, I still am. We just had the most terrible row – the most terrible bloody awful row – about this (*shaking transistor*) being on, and that (*pointing at television with transistor*) being on, and then she went off and I've been sitting here, with them still on, not even hearing, what do you make of that, Japes, eh?

Jason Oh, referred something or other, isn't it called, these days? You know, if you have a pain in your leg, it's actually being referred there from your neck – so if you have a row about noise and then don't do anything about the noise, it's really a referred row – or something. In other words, I can't make anything of it.

Anita (*picking up bag, wallet, keys, etc.*) She's left home for good. Without her keys, her money – (*putting them into bag*) – oh, and her pot and stuff, so she'll be back, won't she? Though will it be for good or for ill, will she be back for good or for ill, is the question? What can I get you, tea, coffee, squash –

Jason I've brought my own. (*taking bottle out of bag*) Saw it in that new health shop in the village, the one with jars of weeds and turds and what have you in the window – and there was this – herbal – costs about three times as much as a bottle of wine – but then I suppose you're meant to keep the bottle to put weeds and turds in –

Anita (*bringing him glass*) I went out to draw, you see. That turned out to be my mistake.

Jason Oh. (*pouring himself a drink*)

Anita (*filling her glass from wine*) Such a beautiful day. And suddenly there was the impulse – it's been years, Japes, honestly, years –

Jason Yes, yes, it must be.

Anita So. So I was very careful. Thoughtful. Dutiful. Reminded her that her half-term was over tomorrow and she still hadn't gone to the library to do her project on – on – some history, King Charles the – one of them – and I was very sweet, I really was, knocked on her door, said, 'Darling, isn't it time you were off? – gave her a couple of quid for her tea – hah, hah! – and said we'd see her for dinner, eating a bit late because of Daddy, about eight-thirty, that all right, darling, all right, darling? (*Smiles ingratiatingly at Jason.*)

   Jason laughs.

So then I went and sorted out my things, one ear cocked, you know, to make sure she'd actually gone, and then I heard the door open and close and – and off I went, with my pad and my pencils, to St Mark's, as a matter of fact, back to my early period, my only period – remember when I used to draw it all the time back then? And anyway, I didn't, I suddenly couldn't, didn't want my pad or my pencils sitting in the sun trying to do something that it would just make me miserable and resentful not being able to do so came back to the house to find her here, also back in the house, lying on this – (*indicating sofa*) – dragging on a joint, with her bloody noise. And it was the – the thought of it, I mean, that she must have loitered about around the corner in the street or something until she'd seen me gone, and then come back and – the television and the tranny and the pot and the whole slatternly, slovenly, rubbishy – and so I went for her, and she went for me – and – (*Gestures*.) – well, no, that's not fair, not fair on me. I tried to do the grown-up crap first, you know, very calm, cold and calm and reasonable, and she grunted, and smirked and sneered – so I got Mychy into it – 'Remember what your father said about kindness, the real meaning of the word' – then I couldn't remember what he said the real meaning of the word was, it was all very complicated, being Mychy. And anyway, anyway, she just sat there, her eyes deliberately glazed and lips – that way she does – (*Pushes her lips out*.) – and that's when I – I hit her, Japes. The thing is – (*Begins to cry*.)

Jason Oh, Neets. (*Goes to her, puts an arm around her*.)

Anita Across the face. Like a punch. A punch. Oh Christ, Japes.

Jason It's OK, it's OK – it'll be all right, you'll see, you'll see.

Anita I wanted to go after her – I wanted to go after her – I really did, but – but –

Jason She'll be back. You'll make it all right. You know, she's not – not bad or anything –

Anita Well, I'm not bad either.

Jason No, of course you're not. You're both good, very good and – and kind actually.

Anita Then why are we so bad, so unkind with each other?

Jason Well, perhaps because you're both more like each other than either of you recognises, eh, Neets? Sometimes when I'm with one of you it's as if I'm with the other, I forget which is which – the same gestures, even the same sort of jokes, you know.

Anita Jokes? She makes jokes with you, does she? How often do you actually see her, Japes?

Jason Well, only during her holidays. And even then she's on school trips or somewhere else, isn't she?

Anita Yes, but when she is here, like now, how often do you see her?

Jason Well, she looks in now and then.

Anita At your flat?

Jason Of course at my flat, Neets. It's no secret – at least I've never made a secret of it.

Anita But perhaps you don't always say, either.

Jason Well, if I don't, it's not deliberately. Why? Do you mind?

Anita Well, what do you joke about? What sort of things do you talk about together, in your flat?

Jason Well, whatever comes up. Whatever's on her mind.

Anita Oh. Like her shrink, you mean?

Jason Well, no, not like her shrink. For one thing, I don't charge, you see.

Anita Do you talk about us?

Jason Which us?

Anita Any two or three of us. Well, do you?

Jason Really, Neets, I've said, she just pops in now and then, and if I'm busy trying to finish an article or don't feel in the mood, I chuck her out, virtually. It's like that, you see.

Anita I suppose I sound jealous, do I?

Jason No, you just sound as if you regret having to be a mother when you'd like to be a friend.

Anita Was that on purpose?

Jason Mmm?

Anita Did you misunderstand me on purpose? I didn't mean jealous of you with her, I mean the other way around.

Jason Then I did misunderstand you, yes. What I love in her is you.

Anita Thank you. That's lovely. Thank you. (*Kisses him.*) You're still tops at that sort of thing, Japes. What a gift. But if you love me in her, why don't I love me in her, too? I mean, if I hate myself, does that mean that I hate her?

Jason You don't hate her.

Anita I do sometimes. Yes.

Jason No. You get angry –

Anita No, of course I don't hate her. Why did I say that? It's anger – of course it's anger. And it's with myself really, you're right about that too, and it probably all comes down to my being frightened.

Jason Frightened?

Anita Well, I'm at that age, you know – it does happen – I could go menopausal any minute, I could be menopausal now, which would explain me a bit, my ups and downs and downs and ups. (*Pours herself more wine.*)

Jason Darling –

Anita Mmmm?

Jason Darling, Neets. (*Shakes his head.*)

Anita Am I drunk?

Jason Well, you soon will be.

Anita And you wouldn't want to see her see me drunk, is that it?

Jason I don't want to see you drunk. And you always hate it afterwards.

Anita You talk as if I do it all the time.

Jason You've done it once or twice recently.

Anita But only with you. Well, mainly only with you. Only sometimes with poor Mychy, he hates it so much – especially if she's around, so never when she's around, honestly, Japes.

Jason I know, Neets. Where is Mychy?

Anita He's doing one of his things, one of his television things. A very, very big one this time.

Jason Oh yes, of course. *Writers of Our Time.*

Anita It's going to make him even more famous. Which means he'll come home all humble and depressed. Isn't it funny how it depresses him – you'd have loved it, success and fame. Perhaps you should each of you have been the other – but then would I have liked that, because then he'd have been here and you'd have been there, being interviewed – would you have liked it that way round, Japes, that's the question, would you, Japes darling? (*Sees Jason's expression.*) Oh, come on, Japes, what's the matter, I'm only talking, you know me, just talking.

Jason Just talking. I wonder why we always say that – 'just talking' – when talking is about as dangerous as driving, probably ruins as many lives, if not more. Really we should set out the same sort of signs – 'sharp curve in next sentence', 'unfortunate joke ahead', 'slippery surface', 'beware soft patches' –

Anita And as for talking under the influence – here, here you are, Japes. Uncle Japes. Take it away. (*Pushes bottle to him.*) Oh, sorry, darling, the smell, I forgot – here, I'll pour it away.

Jason No, I'm perfectly capable.

Turns to pick up stick. As he does so, Anita jerks bottle away from Jason, who almost falls.

Anita Oh, look, it's almost gone, I might as well – darling, are you all right?

Jason Yes, yes, I'm fine.

Anita Well then, you mustn't glower. It never suits you. Remember what you once said to me: at heart, you were a merry man?

Jason Yes. Yes, I am. You're quite right. (*Little pause.*) So you went up to St Mark's to do a drawing?

Anita No, no, I didn't, I told you. I didn't have the nerve, you see.

Jason The nerve?

Anita I think I'll become a friend instead. They're always pushing stuff through the letter box asking – help keep the grounds up, tend the graves, I suppose, that sort of thing. I mean, if I can't draw it again I can – I can – be its friend instead. Just like your mummy. Yours and Mychy's mummy, Japes.

Jason I wish you did more drawings.

Anita Why? So I wouldn't be so bored and such a nuisance –

Jason You have a talent.

Anita That's not what you said back then, when I was being serious and a proper student. You said the only talent I had was as pussy.

Jason No, I didn't. (*Little pause.*) I couldn't have said that. Not ever.

Anita Yes, you did. (*Rubs herself against him, purring.*)

Jason Oh! (*Laughs.*) Yes, yes – (*Strokes her head.*) Well, that's all right then, because it's true – except it wasn't, isn't, your only talent. You can draw. You really can. And if you really can't do St Mark's – well, what about your children's book – the woodlice, wasn't it going to be? Why don't you get back to that, Neets?

Anita Bedbugs actually. Basil and Archie, the Bashful Bedbugs. I burnt them.

Jason Burnt them?

Anita My bedbugs.

Jason Why?

Anita You wouldn't understand. Mychy didn't. Why should you?

Jason Well, you might give me the chance at least.

There is a pause.

Why did you burn your bedbugs, Neets?

Anita Because when you came back in that dreadful state and nearly died on us – on me – when you were in intensive care and were almost gone for ever for three whole days – I made a deal. You see?

Jason A deal? What sort of deal, with whom?

Anita How would I know? But I called him God. I made a deal with – with the God one makes deals with. Up at

St Mark's, as a matter of fact. I wanted to do it inside, on a pew, but the doors were locked, so I did it in the churchyard. I said it aloud, at eleven thirty-seven on the Wednesday night of April the thirteenth. Straight after seeing you lying there dead, as good as, as good as dead.

Jason That if I lived you'd – you'd –

Anita Well, it's the only thing I cared – really cared about that I could renounce, wasn't it? I mean I couldn't renounce Mychy or Wendy, could I? All I had to offer was my bedbugs.

Jason Thank you. But Neets, my darling Neets, it's over, my illness, and I'm here, and you've got a life to live, a talent. Look, Neets, what really brought me back to life was a life-support machine, an exceptionally capable liver specialist called Sapperstein, and just possibly – just possibly – my own will to live. (*Little pause.*) Can't you see what a burden you're putting on me by making me somehow responsible – without even giving me a say in the matter? I would never have been party to such a deal –

Anita Can we stop this now, please, Japes? It's making me feel sick. It's quite simple, quite simple. If you'd died I'd have been lost. You've always been what's kept me going, Japes, even when you were on the other side of the world, you kept me where I am, and if you'd died – I'd have died too. Been dead too – for them. (*Pause.*) And that's all there is to it, all right? All right, Japes?

Jason Of course it's all right. After all, it's not much of a burden, is it, being responsible for your abandoning your talent, insuring your marriage with my brother – not to mention keeping Wendy afloat.

Anita Well, we all have our part to play, don't we? I have to be the wife and mother, and whatever you think and whatever you and Mychy think and whatever you and Mychy and the daughter think, at least I try most of the time, and if I have a rotten afternoon sometimes and ask you to come around – well, I still don't ask for much from you, do I? All things considered, do I?

Jason, after a little pause, shakes his head.

So you can go if you want. I'm all right now.

Jason I don't want to go.

Anita Haven't you got any work to do? You're always saying you've got work to do – all those articles on all those poets in all those magazines – I wish I could read them. I would if I could understand them – funny how I can always understand what Mychy writes, but then he's popular, isn't he? And that's why – that's why he's – (*Gestures.*) – and you're – (*Gestures.*)

Jason Oh, Neets, oh God, Neets!

Anita You think I'm going to do some more drinking.

Jason I hope not. For my sake.

Anita Do I make you want to drink, then?

Jason Not always. But occasionally, when you're like this, I feel an urge to join in.

Anita For old times' sake?

Jason Well, there are only old times because suddenly there are new times.

Anita Really? Really, really, really. New times are afoot, are they, at last, at long last?

Jason I mean – I'm staying for your sake. For everybody's sake. And you're not going to drink for my sake. And that's it, Neets.

Anita My jailer then, is what you plan to be, is it? I think I'll open another bottle and see what happens. (*Heads towards kitchen.*)

Jason hesitates, makes a decision, heads towards door.

(*re-emerging*) Or you can do me a poem. (*Goes to sofa, sits, pats sofa.*) Come on, I promise I'll be good.

Jason, after a moment, goes to sofa, sits down.
Anita moves closer to him.

Go on then.

Jason
Slowly the poison the whole blood stream fills.
It is not the effort nor the failure tires.
The waste remains, the waste remains and kills.

It is not your system of clear sight that mills
Down small to the consequence a life requires;
Slowly the poison the whole blood stream fills.

They bled an old dog dry –

Anita Stop it, Japes! That's not poetry, it's cruelty! Old dog! Poison! You're making it up to punish me.

Jason No, I'm not. And it's a poem all right. I used it as an *aide memoire*.

Anita Do that one – that one – the crying girl one. Simple and faithless – 'La Figlia che – La Figlia che' –

Jason 'La Figlia che Piange'.

Anita 'La Figlia che Piange'. (*Arranges herself, with her head on his lap.*)

Jason
Stand on the highest pavement of the stair,
Lean on a garden urn,

Weave, weave the sunlight in your hair–
Clasp your flowers to you with a pained surprise –
Fling them to the ground and turn
With a fugitive resentment in your eyes:
But weave, weave the sunlight in your hair.

Anita and Jason kiss passionately.

Anita Got you again. Haven't I? Got you. Got you. Got you.

Jason Yes, oh, Neets, Neets, yes.

Lights begin to go down as Anita and Jason make love passionately.
    Lights up on Jason and Anita lying with her head in his lap, both asleep.
    Sound of door opening.

Michael (*off*) Hi, anybody.

Michael enters, looks at them, arranges Anita's clothing, picks up knickers and stuffs them into his pocket. He goes to adjust Jason's clothing.
    Jason is murmuring lines from 'La Figlia che Piange' in his sleep.
    Michael attempts to zip up Jason's fly.
    Jason feels Michael's hand on him, clutches it as he wakes up, stares at Michael.

Cogitations. It's cogitations. Not meditations.

Jason What?

Michael 'La Figlia che Piange'. You were reciting it in your sleep. But you said 'these meditations still surprise', instead of 'these cogitations still surprise' –

Jason Oh. Yes, 'cogitations'. But 'amaze', isn't it? 'These cogitations still amaze' –

Michael 'Amaze'! Yes, you're right. 'Amaze'. 'These cogitations still amaze / The troubled midnight' – two completely different conditions, really, 'surprise' being a kind of shock to the system, a being taken out of, while 'amaze' is – a growing, a growing sense of – (*Gestures.*) Oh, where's Wendy?

Jason Actually, she's at my place. Or was the last time I saw her. She turned up suddenly, in a bit of a state, she'd had a spat with – (*Nods.*) you see, and – so forth.

Michael Oh. (*Nods.*) What about, did she say?

Jason No, well, before she could get into it properly –

Anita (*moving in sleep*) Japes, Japes –

Jason (*nods*) – phoned, and asked me to come over, so I got her version instead. As far as I could make out it was to do with transistors being on, television being on, school projects not being attended to – anyway, she's still in my flat, our Wendy, or was when last seen.

Anita (*moans out in her sleep*) No – no – (*mumblingly*) Mychy –

Jason I think it's for you.

Michael Ah. There, there, darling. There, there, I'm here. (*going to her, patting her gently*) She's such a – such a lovely – when she's asleep. This little frown, have you noticed?

Jason Yes. Actually, my good leg's going – do you think you could –

Michael Oh, right, here. (*Takes Jason's place, except with his arm around her shoulder.*) Goodness, she's gone again, isn't she? Completely out. Would you mind –

Jason takes Michael's glass, pours Scotch into it. As he does so, takes a quick sniff at the drink, feels it deep in his soul, brings glass back to Michael.

Do you think I should get her to bed? Well, what else did you talk about, the two of you, apart from the usual Wendy?

Jason I can't really remember – oh, yes, I asked her about her children's book –

Michael Bedbugs! She talked about her bedbugs, did she? Well, that's good, being able to talk about it means she must be getting over it at last, the humiliation of it. Poor old Neets. (*Strokes her cheek.*)

Jason Humiliation?

Michael Well – (*checking to make sure Anita's still gone, lowering his voice slightly*) – that's how she saw it as, failure and humiliation, although Weedon claimed he never actually rejected it outright – the worst he'd been was mildly discouraging, according to him, but the fact is that whatever he said, he completely undermined her confidence. Did she tell you about what she did with it? All of it?

Jason She said she'd burnt it.

Michael Burnt them? Is that what she told you? No, no, she didn't burn them, she taxied drunkenly home from her lunch with Weedon, and tried to flush them down the lavatory. I found her up to her ankles in water, pulling away at the chain, sobbing and screaming out, well, curses really, curses on Weedon, on her bedbugs, on everything, everyone, all of us, her whole life. Since then, she's refused to discuss it, gets quite hysterical when I mention it – but if she's started with you – that could be a good sign, she might be thinking of getting down to it again, eh? But as for Weedon – what was it you called him once? Oh, yes – fuckwit. He's a complete fuckwit. You should have heard him this afternoon. After that interview. But then I shouldn't have agreed to do it, should I? My own fault entirely. I let him bully me into it. So it's because of him that next month there I'll be, in a million homes, think of it, a million and a half, actually, dilating on the theme of my fictions, the recurrent themes, like recurrent colds or sore throats or prison sentences – no, that's concurrent, isn't it – anyway, loss, loss and betrayal, my recurrent themes, with an occasional whiff of redemption. He could sniff it, he said, sniff the whiff of redemption on my prose. On my latest prose. But actually I don't think it's redemption, more an acceptance, an infomed acceptance of the nature of things.

Jason Mychy, I think I'd better go.

Michael Could you give us a hand, just to get her to her feet?

Jason No, I mean go away. I've been thinking of it for quite a while now. Of going away for a bit.

Michael (*after a little pause*) How long a bit?

Jason I don't know. For quite a bit, I expect.

Michael Well, not for good, you don't mean? (*Little pause.*) But where would you go? Not back to Guyana, for God's sake! I won't allow it, Japes.

Jason No, nowhere warm, don't worry. In fact I wouldn't mind trying somewhere really cold. Icy even. With stiff winds. Might get me back to some real writing again, a hostile climate. Do we know anything about Nova Scotia?

Michael Nova Scotia? Canada. East coast. Near where the *Titanic* went down. You'd hate it. Look, Japes, what

I've really been trying to say – don't you understand what
I'm trying to say? That it's all right, you see. It really is.

Jason What is?

Michael I don't mind. That's what I'm saying. I don't
mind.

Jason Don't mind what?

Michael That you've started again. (*Little pause.*) I mean,
here we are, we've reached this stage of – of, well, our
lives with each other. These could be good years, good
years, why shouldn't they be? Here. Together. As we used
to be, but – but grown-up. A little grown-up, anyway.
That's the point, Japes. (*Little pause.*) We need you, is
also the point. She needs you. Desperately needs you.
As do I. Is the point.

Jason But it's time I learnt not to need you, either of you
is the point, Mychy, for me. I've got to go. You see.

Anita (*waking up*) Mychy, Mychy. (*looking vaguely
towards Jason*)

Michael Actually, I'm here, Neets.

Anita Oh. Oh, so you are. I knew you were, the two of
you, I could hear your voices winding about in my sleep.
Well, what's been going on – (*getting up shakily*) – what
have you been talking about?

Michael Actually, Japes has just been saying that he's
going away.

Anita Going away?

Michael To Nova Scotia, he thinks.

Anita Nova Scotia.

Jason It's near where the *Titanic* went down.

There is a ring on the doorbell.

Michael Who the hell is that?

Jason Wendy, isn't it? She forgot her keys, didn't you say?

Michael Oh. Well, I'll go and – and – (*Goes to door, off.*)

Jason and Anita look at each other. Jason turns away, picks up Michael's drink, lifts it.

Wendy (*voice off, inaudible*)

Michael (*off*) Don't be silly, darling, of course we want you, come in.

Jason puts the glass down firmly, looks at Anita.

Anita You can't.

Michael (*off*) Oh, for heaven's sake, Wendy, nobody's going to eat you, I promise!

Anita I won't let you.

Lights.

SCENE TWO

The same. Ten years later. Spring. Early afternoon. There is an up-to-date television. A high chair by the table. Toys in evidence, scattered. On the table, remnants of lunch. The television is on, a children's programme, possibly a cartoon, in progress.

Anita, in apron, enters. She clears the rest of the table, carries plates off, hurriedly. She returns, looks around, picks up toys, puts them out of sight, moves the high chair to a less conspicuous position, looks around the room anxiously, checking, then goes to Wendy's/Jason's

*old room. It is very tidy, as if for a guest. She checks
herself in the mirror, addresses her hair etc., remembers
her apron, takes it off, goes off to kitchen, enters living
room, makes a sudden decision, scatters the toys roughly
where they were, pulls the high chair back into position.*

   *The front door bell rings. Anita freezes, checks herself
quickly, nearly goes off, notices television is on, turns it
off, goes off.*

Jason (*off*) My dear!

Anita (*off*) Come in, come in!

   Jason enters, followed by Anita.

Jason You looked surprised to see me, am I early?

Anita No, no – well, I was hoping to tidy up before you
got here, excuse the shambles.

Jason No, it looks very charming. As if you've been
having a lively time of it.

Anita It's always lively when they're here.

Jason And are they here often?

Anita Every day, almost. She drops them off first thing
in the morning and picks them up after tea – she got
away early today, so she's taken them up to the heath for
a romp. Such a lovely afternoon, for once.

Jason Yes, isn't it?

Anita But you're used to lovely days.

Jason Yes, but they're not English lovely days, they're
French lovely days. Quite different. I haven't had a day
like this for – what, ten and a half years.

Anita Has it been that long? Yes, it has, hasn't it? Christ!

Jason Yes. Christ. So. So Neets the Granny. Granny Neets – you like it, obviously.

Anita I adore it. Much the simplest relationship I've ever had. Perhaps because I've learnt how to say no, and mean it. Actually, it turns out to be quite easy. If you do it from the beginning you can just keep going. At least with the grandchildren. I still haven't tried with the daughter. (*Laughs.*)

Jason But she likes being a mother, does she?

Anita Why shouldn't she? There's nothing to it, really, when she has me as the grandmother. Actually, that's not fair, it's all a little difficult for her, she takes her work very seriously and they're at the age when they have to be watched every minute – they're Nigel and Alexander, by the way, did I say in my letter? Two and three – nearly four, Alexander, next month.

Jason What does she do, Wendy? You didn't say that in your letter, either.

Anita Didn't I? No, well, I just wanted to stick to the main – the main event – well, she's a social worker, our Wendy.

Jason Ah. (*Laughs.*)

Anita (*after a short pause, also laughs*) Yes, I know. Her particular passion is abused children. She's completely fearless – going into the most dreadful places. She's been attacked and hit, threatened with knives – the sort of thing one used to read about in the papers. Well, not read about – but vaguely took in, as one turned the pages. I'm very proud of her. Not that I have any right to be – she did it all in spite of me.

Jason I take it there isn't a husband. Husband figure – (*Gestures.*) – a father. On the scene.

Anita No, just Daniel. He wants to be a television director. He's a nice young man – just completely useless when it comes to his responsibilities. He comes around now and then, for Sunday lunch, plays with them charmingly – but he doesn't want more than that. And isn't really wanted more than that.

Jason (*after a little pause*). And where's Mychy?

Anita In his study. Working.

Jason Ah. I won't disturb him then.

Anita No. Better not. But he'll be out quite soon, I expect, wanting his tea. You'll see him then. And Wendy and the boys too, I hope – the boys are usually a bit fractious and also wanting their tea, especially Nigel. But I haven't offered you anything, Jason, tea, coffee – I assume you've eaten.

Jason Oh yes. Copiously, thank you. Enormous lunch.

Anita Really? So you've got an appetite at last. Yes, I can see you have – it suits you.

Jason Thank you.

Anita Where did you go?

Jason Mmm?

Anita Where did you have lunch?

Jason Oh, that place off St Martin's Lane. The Ivy, I think it's – um – actually I wouldn't mind a small brandy, if there is one?

Anita (*gesturing to table*) Oh, there might be, see what there is. The Ivy, eh? I haven't been there since oh – since Mychy – You've become so successful, Japes.

Jason Well, I don't know – if I am it's all a bit late, quite bewildering really, I wish I'd had some practice. Have you read any of them?

Anita I read the first. I expect it would have made me laugh even more, if I hadn't known us so well.

Jason I didn't think of it as autobiographical.

Anita No, more as biographical, really. (*Laughs.*) I didn't mind – after all you very sweetly set me in my context – and nothing in the book was unkind.

Jason It certainly wasn't intended to be. In fact here and there its generosity was commented on. Its generous-heartedness.

> *They look at each other. Both laugh.*

There you are, Neets.

Anita And there you are, Japes. One of the reviews that caught my eye said that you could feel – positively feel – your love of women.

Jason No. No it didn't. It said my love of a particular woman. The one I wrote about.

Anita Are you writing more?

Jason And more and more. Now I've started at last I intend never to stop.

Anita Well, why should you? And you look so well on it. Your stick? Where's your stick?

Jason There's a new operation. I had it done in Nice four, no five, years ago.

Anita And you're drinking.

Jason Yes. But not enough.

Anita To make a difference.

Jason Oh yes. Enough to make a difference, otherwise what would be the point? But not enough to mess anything up. Anything important.

Anita So there you are then.

Jason I miss you.

Anita That's good. Or what would have been the point?

Jason You look as lovely as I've imagined you.

Anita You must have imagined the ten years then, because I show them, every day of them.

Jason Have they been very cruel?

Anita I went to pieces after you left. Even more to pieces – Mychy got me into a clinic at last. He had to do things – come to counselling sessions, talk about himself to professional friends, God, how he must have hated that, and of course support me for hours on end for days on end sometimes – but he stuck it out and made me stick it out – and brought my daughter to me. And she brought me Nigel and Alexander – and if it was cruel, I've still ended up with more than I deserve, haven't I? (*Her voice is shaking, close to tears.*) Mychy's doing.

Jason You deserve everything good –

Anita Don't, Japes!

Jason goes to her, puts his arms around her.

They embrace.

(*separating*). Perhaps I'll have a drop – just a tiny drop – it smells as if I need it. I do, sometimes. But not often. (*Smiles.*)

Jason Here. (*Hands her his glass, goes to table, pours himself another small one.*)

Anita Well, what a couple we are now.

They toast each other. They sit in silence.

Jason Here's a question. Did you – does Mychy know?

Anita About what?

Jason About Wendy?

Anita Oh. She's Michael's, of course.

Jason Why of course?

Anita I don't know. (*Laughs.*) Well then, perhaps she's yours. The truth is, I stopped thinking about it long ago – it's the boys now, you see.

Jason And you're the grandmother, whichever way around it might have been, yes, I do see. Quite.

Anita Does it matter to you, then? Because you can choose to be whichever you want, really, can't you? Father or uncle? As long as you keep it to yourself.

Jason You see – (*Stops himself.*) Thank you.

They smile at each other.

Anita Tell me about your life in Antibes.

Jason It's very simple. I get up late, have breakfast on my terrace if the weather's OK, which it usually is, potter about in my study until I'm ready to write. Then I write for a couple of hours. Then I walk into town, and have lunch. Then I walk along the front, whatever the weather. Go home. Read. Then a nap. Have an aperitif. Then either eat in or go to friends for dinner, or meet them in a restaurant. Then home. Potter about in my study. And then towards midnight I begin to write. And go on until

I'm in danger of getting overexcited. Take my sleeping pills. Go to bed.

Anita It sounds rather monastic. Luxuriously monastic.

Jason Not really. There are people – some of them I've become close to.

Anita Is it a big flat?

Jason Preposterously big. It's got seven rooms, not counting the necessary ones. And the terrace is enormous. View of the sea.

Anita You love it.

Jason I do.

Anita Do you realise I've spent all my adult life in this house?

Jason So you have.

Anita I don't know any more if I love it, but I could never live anywhere else. And of course Mychy's spent his whole life –

Jason So he has. I never felt much about it – it was always the people that were in it –

Anita It's still yours, half of it.

Jason So it is. But it's not, is it, in any way that matters? It's yours, my half. I'll sort it out as soon as I get home.

Anita Thank you, Japes.

Jason That's all settled then.

Anita I'll ask Wendy to move in. They live in a really miserable little place in Holloway, dreadful for the boys, great lorries thundering past day and night and no parks or decent walks.

Jason (*after a little pause*) Will there be enough room?

Anita Well, there will if – if Mychy comes to you.

Jason He can't. I'm sorry, Neets.

Anita But you haven't even thought it over.

Jason Yes, I have. I was pretty sure from your letter that you'd ask.

Anita But why not? With all those rooms, surely – and you could afford the staff –

Jason I'm getting married, you see. And she's got two children. Teenagers. They're delightful and I'm very fond of them – but they're boisterous. I'll need the rooms. And because she's pregnant.

Anita Well, certainly not so monastic then. But how wonderful, Japes. I'm very happy for you.

Jason Thank you.

Anita (*goes to him, kisses him*) Congratulations.

Jason Thank you.

Anita Who is she, may I ask?

Jason She's American. Divorced. She's very young – well, by my standards. But then she started very young and I'm starting rather late.

Anita But you love her.

Jason I hope so. I shall do my best by her.

Michael's study opens. Michael stands looking at Jason and Anita, withdraws into his study, closes the door. There is a slight pause. The door opens again. Brisk footsteps. Michael enters. He is very neatly dressed, and is wearing a beret on his head. He has a small beard.

Michael (*going straight to Anita*) My dear, my dear, here I am.

Anita Mychy, Japes is here. (*Turns, guides him towards Jason.*)

Michael and Japes stand staring at each other.

Michael Japes? How do you do, Japes?

Jason How do you do. How do you do, Mychy?

Michael Thank you, thank you. (*Stares at Jason.*) I've been thinking about my new novel. It will have twenty-seven chapters. Twenty-seven pages each chapter. Beige covers. A photograph of myself on the back. On the front the number twenty-seven. Possibly twenty-eight. What do you think?

Jason It sounds very interesting.

Michael What? What do you think?

Jason I think it will be very interesting, Mychy.

Michael Interesting. Interesting. Have you seen this? (*Unzips his fly.*) This is interesting, I think it is.

Anita (*goes to him, takes his arm*) Tea, Mychy. (*Zips up his fly.*) Time for your tea. (*Leads him to sofa.*)

Michael Yes, tea. And a pastry. A pastry would be perfect.

Anita Yes. A pastry would be perfect. (*Takes off his beret, strokes his head briefly.*)

Michael rubs the place that Anita has rubbed, turns on television.

You see. With the boys growing up – they can't move in –

Jason No, I'll talk to Tishy. There's bound to be a place – a home of some sort – perhaps in Nice or – somewhere near –

Anita Thank you. Thank you, Japes. Oh, they're back – (*a sudden sound of doors, children's voices, etc., from kitchen*) – and wanting their tea too, I expect. I'll tell Wendy you're here.

> *Jason looks at Michael, hesitates, goes and sits beside him, on sofa.*
> *Michael looks at Jason, nods, smiles, stares at television.*
> *Jason puts his arm tentatively around Michael's shoulder.*
> *After a moment, Michael removes Jason's arm. They sit.*
> *Off, Anita's voice, laughter, children.*
> *Lights.*

MICHAEL

Characters

Jason

Wendy

Michael

Anita

SCENE ONE

The living room of a house in Hampstead. Evening.
  Wendy, slightly dishevelled, is sitting in the corner
of the sofa, rolling a joint, sipping from glass.
  Sound of front door opening and closing.
  Jason tentatively puts his head around door. He is
carrying a carrier bag.

Jason It's only your old Uncle Jason, child molester.
(*Puts carrier bag on table, sits down beside her.*) How
are you?

  Wendy shrugs, passes him the joint. He takes it, they
  pass it back and forth as they talk.

I'm a bit early, I think, did I nearly interrupt something?

Wendy Nothing much. (*imitating adult*) Nothing of any
consequence.

Jason Oh, good. I met a young man on the doorstep,
I hope I didn't frighten him off.

Wendy No. I'd already done that. (*Laughs.*)

Jason Yes, well, he did look a trifle disorganised – red in
the face, and I thought I noticed some buttons undone.

Wendy His name's Dominic. Dominic Wanker.

Jason Not one of the Shropshire Wankers, by any chance?

  Wendy laughs. They smoke a while.

The suspense – I'm not sure I can endure it.

Wendy Why do you want to know?

Jason You're my little niece. I take an interest.

Wendy Well, he only stayed twenty minutes.

Jason Still, twenty minutes can be a long time in matters of the heart. Whole lives born out of them.

Wendy Well, he kissed me. And I kissed him back. And we got going for a bit and then he sort of froze, and started asking me questions about my age. I mean, he's only nineteen himself, well, that's what he says, but I bet he's eighteen really, and I told him I was seventeen so he'd know it was all right – I look seventeen, don't I, Japes?

Jason Yes, you do. Or younger even. Perhaps even fifteen.

Wendy That's because you know. And then he wanted to know was the house really empty, where was my mum and dad – mum and dad he called them. I said you'll see them later on the television, live as life – you can look at them on the screen over there while we're doing it on the sofa over here, you couldn't be safer than that, could you?

Jason And this didn't appeal to him?

Wendy He said he hadn't come here for this sort of thing, he said as far as he was concerned I'd only invited him back for a cup of tea and talk about books, and I said, come on, I said, come on, Dominic, you started it, you kissed me and you put your hand on my bum, and he said well, yes, that's as far as he meant it to go, it didn't mean he wanted me swarming all over him, and he had plans for the evening anyway. And he went. And you came. And that's all. (*Laughs*.) You know he was the only one I could get, out of the whole lot of them at the Ginger Cat – I sat there hours and hours and there were some – one or two – who looked – looked – well, you know. As if they could – could talk, at least. But he was the only one I had the nerve to look at and smile at and nod to, because I could see he was pathetic and you know what my problem is. I'm not – not exactly attractive, that's what my problem is. Look at me.

Jason You're very attractive, so that's not your problem.

Wendy Well, what is it then?

Jason Your problem is that you're fifteen and you think you should want things you don't really want.

Wendy Like sex, you mean?

Jason Like sex, I mean.

Wendy How do you know whether I want it or not?

Jason How would you feel if you'd just had it with young Wanker Dominic?

Wendy How would I know, that's what I was trying to find out? Do you think I'd have lost my self-respect, then?

Jason You'd have lost mine.

Wendy I wouldn't have told you.

Jason I'd have known anyway.

Wendy How?

Jason I'm your Uncle Japes. I know your every impulse, I share in your every humiliation – that's one of the burdens I carry through life –

Wendy Oh, good. Then I'm going to put you through it, Uncle Japes.

Jason Be careful. I have a weak heart.

Wendy (*alarmed*) Have you really?

Jason I have as far as you're concerned. (*Gets up, takes bottle from carrier bag.*)

Wendy What's that?

Jason Elderflower. (*Going to drinks table, pours himself a glass.*)

Wendy Really? What year?

Jason It doesn't say, so it's plonk. Elderflower plonk. (*Goes over to television, pokes tentatively at a button.*) I can never get this bloody thing to work, isn't it almost time? (*gesturing Wendy towards set*)

Wendy (*takes Jason's wrist, looks at his watch*) It doesn't even begin for another ten minutes, and then there'll be all the introductions and speeches and rubbish – Japes?

Jason Mmm?

Wendy is lighting another joint.

That's your last of the evening, my girl.

Wendy Why are you called Japes, anyway, old Uncle Japes? (*Sits down, back against his knees.*)

Jason Oh. Well – actually, because of you. Whenever your parents couldn't get you to bed they'd ask me to do it, so I'd chase you around the house, being your bogeyman, and you'd laugh and scream and beg me to stop it, oh, stop, Uncle Jason, oh Uncle Jason, please! And sometimes it came out Japes instead of Jason, and it began to stick. So in a sense you christened me. Invented me. Made me what I've been ever since. Well, to those who love me. My friends.

Wendy Japes.

Jason Japes indeed.

Wendy Were you in love with Mummy?

Jason Of course. Always.

Wendy And are you still?

Jason I said always.

Wendy Oh – oh, I see. That sort of love. Devotion.

Jason Exactly. That sort.

Wendy Doesn't sound like you.

Jason Doesn't it? And how would you know what sounds like me?

Wendy Well, I know the sort of things you did when you were out in Guyana, they used to talk about what you got up to, and your drinking – you were drunk all the time, from the way they talked.

Jason Ah well. Those were my dog days.

Wendy Wish I'd been there with you, out in Guyana with you, in your dog days.

Jason Look at me.

Wendy (*looks up into his face*) Well? What?

Jason This is what's left of me from my dog days.

Wendy (*still looking*) You look – you look all right, to me, as a matter of fact, Japes. If Wanker Dominic had your eyes, all sharp and bleary, or these nice puffy cheeks – (*Pats his cheek.*) – and those lovely wrinkles on his brow –

Jason Then he'd probably be unemployable, like me, pensioned off into oblivion before his prime, like me, because these puffs and wrinkles, my girl, these bleary eyes –

Wendy Those bleary eyes – *she sings it as she hands him her joint. He sucks in, hands it back.*

Jason (*sucking in, singing*) These bleary eyes –

Wendy *and* **Jason** (*singing*) These/Those bleary eyes –

Jason This is how I was those last months. Now you listen to me, my girl. It was like this. You listen to me. Are you listening? (*Tilts her head up.*)

Wendy (*staring straight into his eyes*) I am. Yes. Yes, I am, Japes.

Jason I was drinking so much that I became professionally incompetent. When I gave lectures I slurred my words, tottered about, fell down. The students complained, their parents complained, even the police complained, they got so sick of picking me up from the pavements and gutters and drying me out in their cells – (*Little pause.*) After they sacked me they had to ban me from the campus – I used to hang about outside the gates, crying to be let back in. I'd stop colleagues and promise them I'd be good if only they'd let me into my office, and into the common room, to sit at the bar again, on my old stool, just for an hour. Just for an hour. I promise I won't be a nuisance, I promise, promise, please, please – If you'd seen me, my girl, and smelt me, you wouldn't have wished to be with me, not anywhere near me. I'd be dead now, months dead, if your father hadn't come out and brought me home. And now – (*Stubs out joint.*) – I'm just beginning – just beginning to get a clarity, a degree of clarity – at least enough to see that it's important, now, here, this minute – that you should be clear too. About me.

Wendy is rolling another joint.

No, you're not having another one! Haven't you heard a word I said? Give it to me.

Wendy If I do I'll take something else instead. I've got some acid.

Jason Acid.

Wendy Remember that dinner party the other evening, for Dad's American publisher and his Italian translator and some bishops for Mum because she wanted to grease them into helping her save every nook and cranny of her darling little St Mark's –

Jason I remember it perfectly well. I was there.

Wendy Were you, Japes? Well, I don't remember you, I really don't. I only remember Mum and Dad before they all came, telling me how I was to behave and the usual crap – but I don't remember the dinner and the rest of it, not at all, I was somewhere different, seeing different, better, funnier, wiser people, with lovely colours all around them, and cats on their knees, and there were friendly snakes curled around some of their necks, and afterwards, all Mummy said was how pleasant it was to see me enjoying myself with their friends for once, not a single scowl all evening – (*Squeals with laughter, sucking on her joint.*) – and Daddy said I had a lovely smile, we should see it more often.

> *Jason reaches to take joint from Wendy. Wendy nips up, dodges away.*

Jason (*gets up, picks up stick*) Give it to me. (*Holds out his hand.*) All of it.

> *Wendy shakes her head.*

(*in a sudden, terrifying roar*) Give it to me, you little shit!

> *Wendy, after a pause, stubs out joint.*

All of it.

Wendy puts joint stuff into his hand.

If I ever find you on acid or anything other than this I'll beat the hell out of you. And that goes for hard booze too, my girl.

Wendy (*knowingly*) But you won't tell them, will you?

Jason What would be the point? They love you too much to beat you. They'd just send you to a shrink.

Wendy You wouldn't beat me.

Jason Wouldn't I? (*Whacks her across a buttock.*)

Wendy screams in pain.
There is a pause.

Sorry. Sorry. Wendy. I didn't mean it to hurt.

Wendy stares at him, turns, runs out.

(*going after her*) Wendy – Wenders –

Sound off of door slamming. Jason stands for a moment, then goes to drinks table, picks up a bottle of whisky, makes as if to pour it, stops himself. Goes back, sees Wendy's stuff, begins to roll a joint.
Lights.

SCENE TWO

The same. Three hours later. Evening. Jason is slumped in armchair, asleep. On TV, La Grande Illusion is coming to the end, music.
Anita enters, in evening dress, carrying statuette. She stands, looking at Jason.

Jason (*waking*) Oh – oh, Wenders, something I was going to say, clear the ashtray, don't forget to clear the – (*Sees*

Anita as she glances at ashtray.) Oh, it's you, hi, Neets. (*Sees the television.*) Oh – *La Grande Illusion*! Such a lovely film, my favourite twenty years ago, probably still is, but can't be sure as I seem to have slept through it, eh? (*Rises slightly groggily, goes to television, fails to turn it off.*) But I'm sure that part of oneself never changes, the *La Grande Illusion*-loving self – damn, what am I doing wrong! (*as he jumps from channel to channel, also in volume*)

Anita Not turning the off-thing, it's down here, see. (*doing it*)

Jason (*seeing statuette*) Oh, that's it, is it, in the metal. Can I see? (*Takes it from Anita.*) Christ, it's heavy.

Anita Yes, Mychy nearly dropped it. The others seemed prepared, they held it clamped to their chests.

Jason Probably afraid they'd try and take it back. (*studying statuette*)

Anita Yes, well, Mychy held it by its neck, here, like this – (*taking it back, almost dropping it. She is clearly pissed.*) Ooops – like one of those discus-throwers –

Jason Yes, yes, I saw, swinging it slightly too, would have been menacing if it hadn't been for his speech, very charming, very adroit, very modest, and scarcely a single thank you, was there? Apart from to you.

Anita For my usual patience.

Jason Usual beautiful patience.

Anita Yes. (*Giggles.*) Didn't he look – didn't he look so – (*Gestures.*)

Jason Yes. The very picture of the chap who won the best, um, well the –

Anita Yes, better not go into that, rather a sore point it turns out, just general congratulations.

Jason Yes, yes, I did wonder – but where is he?

Anita Gone for a little stroll. To clear his head. To sort it out. (*Gestures.*) To think it through.

Jason To think what through?

Anita He didn't say, but life, death, all the big and even medium-sized questions, God, I need a pee. (*Goes out.*)

> *Jason picks up statuette, studies it, laughs, glances around nervously, suddenly sees ashtrays, puts down statuette, picks up ashtrays, looks desperately around for somewhere to empty them.*
> *Michael enters, in dinner jacket. He is also pissed.*

Jason Ah, it's our award-winning –

Michael What are you doing with them? Weighing them?

Jason (*laughs*) No, just emptying them. (*Looks for waste-paper basket, can't see it.*)

Michael What did she think?

Jason Who?

Michael About her father. On television. Receiving that. (*Gesturing to statuette.*) Did she make any comments, have any views?

Jason Ah. Well, actually – (*giving up, putting ashtrays down*) – she rushed off just before it started, think she suddenly decided to watch you with someone else, one of her friends, much more exciting to be able to say, 'Hey, that's my dad' – and you were terrific, Mychy, Anita and I were just saying.

Michael Yes, didn't I behave well? (*Laughs.*) Impeccably.
Modest too, I thought – said my thank-yous to Neets
very becomingly – perhaps I shouldn't have left you out,
or Wendy, or my various agents, past and present, but
then one can't include everybody, can one, or one would
find oneself going back to Mummy and Daddy, formative
schoolmasters, early influences – Shakespeare, Molière,
Chekhov, Ibsen, Corneille, Racine, Webster, Tourneur,
Ford, and – and all the rest of them, I think I'll go out.

Jason You've only just come in.

Michael That's true. But I think I'll go back out. I'm not
really ready, you see, Japes, old cheese.

Jason Ready for what?

Michael To be at home.

Jason Ah, the drink. (*Laughs sympathetically.*) Yes.
I remember those times.

Michael I don't. No, I really don't. I don't remember any
time that being drunk stopped you from being at home.
My home anyway. What am I talking about, what do
I mean, my home? Our home, it's our home – always has
been, always will – isn't that right? Sorry there isn't room
for you any more –

Jason What are you talking about, Mychy?

Michael I'm talking about shoving you into a little
granny flat around the corner and out of sight. Though
of course you're not out of sight, you're here, in sight,
but you sleep out of sight, you have to go away and
come back again and again – to your own home. Well,
to your own half of your own home.

Jason I'm very happy in my flat, Mychy. It's very
comfortable and I like being in it. (*making to go*) But if
you're asking me to leave –

Michael Asking you to leave? Don't be an ass. What's the matter with you? I've just told you, I'm the one who's leaving. Going back out. (*Goes out.*)

Jason looks after him, sound of door opening and closing, then picks up statuette, reads inscription again, laughs, suddenly remembers ashtrays, picks them up.

Anita (*enters*) Oh. I thought I heard Mychy.

Jason Yes, well, he just popped in. To touch base. I think he's a bit upset that Wendy didn't watch him on television. Here, anyway. I said she'd probably gone to see it with one of her friends.

Anita Friends? She hasn't got any friends, she's just a hanger-on, a hanger-on to a gang of pot-heads and layabouts at that awful little coffee dump –

Jason The Cheshire Cat. (*putting ashtray down discreetly*)

Anita What? (*Looking around irritably, sees ashtrays.*)

Jason It's called the Cheshire – no, it's not, it's the –

Anita (*picking up ashtrays*) Five, she smoked five bloody joints –!

Jason Actually a couple of them are mine.

Anita What? You smoke joints with Wendy!

Jason Well, no, actually I think it was after Wendy. We were talking, you see – (*Gestures.*) – and then she left and I saw her stuff there and suddenly an old impulse –

Anita Talking, were you? I didn't know she could do that. What were you talking about?

184

Jason Oh, just life and love and the whole damn thing. You know.

Anita Really? No, I don't. I don't know. But then she never says a word to me about anything – how do you manage it?

Jason Oh well – a fresh face but a familiar figure – of the family but not in it, I suppose – (*Gestures.*)

Anita And boyfriends? Does she talk to you about boys? Whether there is one, for instance?

Jason Oh, nothing that intimate, good heavens – I'm sure there's nothing – nobody to worry about –

Anita How can one help worrying when she's so – so – feckless – (*emptying ashtrays*) – it's not just that she isn't here when we get back or didn't even bother to watch her father on one of the most important – (*Gestures.*) – but that she leaves a trail to mark her absence, so in the end that's what the evening becomes, a rotting trail of her not being. Or being not. And if I try to tell her anything, anything at all about life, and consequences, the awful bloody consequences tomorrow of what you're doing or not doing today – (*pouring herself a drink*) – and it doesn't matter what tone I adopt, how tender – tender and careful I am, she just sits there, or lies there in bed in her pit of a bedroom, gaping away from me, her eyes dead, either stoned or deliberately, quite deliberately, making herself into an idiot, a deaf idiot, and really I might as well do as I actually feel – and shriek and scream and shake her and shake her. At least I'd give myself a really good time, and who knows, it might do some good, she'd know how much I care – care – (*Laughs.*) 'Teach me to care and not to care' – isn't that the quote? Michael's favourite quote, how does it go on?

Jason 'Teach me to sit still.'

Anita Ah. Ahah! 'Teach me to care and not to care and teach my daughter to sit still.' That would do it, wouldn't it?

Jason Well, I don't expect you can teach her to sit still, at her age. She'll have to find out how to do that by herself, won't she? And it won't be for a long time yet, I shouldn't think, and you know, if I may say, from my very limited acquaintance with her, she seems a very lively, healthy, intelligent, balanced girl – altogether a chip off the old block.

Anita Really? Which block?

Jason Ah! (*Laughs.*) Your block. It was your block I was thinking of – and you know, Neets, perhaps you should give it a go, teaching yourself not to care – why not? Your caring isn't going to make her change and you have a life apart from her, you and Mychy, the two of you – separately and together, but apart from her.

Anita Separately and together. Christ, that sounds good. Separately and together. Well, let's see – separately – separately, I keep the churchyard in order. Do a bit of drawing, tend the church, that's my life separately. Together, I sit beside my husband when he's getting a prize, and talk to him about a daughter that's never there to talk to. That's it, that's me. Separately and together. (*Laughs.*) And how are you doing, Uncle Jason, separately and together?

Jason As you see me, my dear.

Anita Your what? You've never called me my dear before. Not ever.

Jason You've never called me uncle before. Not ever. But perhaps both terms are appropriate to us as we are now.

A routine endearment for an established routine. Uncle me and my dear you.

Anita But my dear uncle, you're not being at all routine. (*looking at Jason*) You look – what do you look? You look different. Alive, would it be? Well, there's a bit of a gleam in your eye that looks like life. Very like life. Of course it could just come from smoking pot and moving in the younger set. But I haven't seen it since – since –

Jason I was dead.

Anita Well, you were never actually dead, were you? I mean you just popped in and out. Like Mychy just now. A brief visit was all it amounted to.

Jason Yes, but even a brief visit can have a lingering effect. Old Lazarus – young Lazarus he was – young Lazarus didn't just get up and strut about as if he'd had a nap, in fact he probably felt like death for a long time. Probably the rest of his life. But as you say, mine was a brief visit, so –

Anita So you're back, are you? Old Uncle Jason is turning into young Japes.

Jason Or the old Japes. Of fond memory.

They look at each other, laugh slightly.

Anita And does old Japes want a drink again too?

Jason Yes.

Anita But he won't, will he?

Jason No.

Anita What does it feel like, not drinking?

Jason Well, the last time I was drinking I was drinking three bottles of rum a day and I have no idea what that felt like, it was in another country.

Anita But what do you feel like now?

Jason Now? This minute, you mean?

Anita Now generally. Day-to-day now.

Jason Ah. Well, yesterday and all the days before that I felt like Uncle Jason. But now, today – this minute – well, of fond memory –

Anita Fond memory of drinking?

Jason No. Of your saying I made love better than any man ever in your whole life.

Anita Did I say that?

Jason (*pointing to ceiling*) There. In that room up there, you said it. Don't you remember?

Anita I do. But it was a different room then. Eighteen years ago. It was your room. Another country.

Jason Yes, but we don't need visas or passports to get to it. It's still there if you close your eyes. Go on then, close them. (*Little pause.*) Close them. Go on. I dare you, Neets.

 Anita takes a drink, closes her eyes.

Now, see – see? There I am, lying on the bed, naked. And you're sitting at the end of the bed, naked. And your hair down to your shoulders. And your eyes full of tears. Because I'm crying. I'm crying because I'm happy and I'm frightened. And because I know that whenever I cry it makes you cry. And I love that. But I always pretend that it's my leg that makes me cry, and that you only make love with me because you're sorry for me. And you always say, 'No, no, my darling, no, no, I love you and I love everything about you and above all I love your leg,' and you stroke it and you kiss it and you say,

'Poor brave leg, poor brave beautiful leg, I love it so,' and then we make love and then you say, 'You make love to me better than any man I've ever known. No man can ever make love to me as you do.'

Anita, after a pause, opens her eyes, gets up, goes to table, pours herself a drink.

Why don't you ever come to see me in my flat any more? I watch you going past almost every morning from my window. You never even look up. But you know I'm there, don't you? Why don't you look up ever? Why don't you ever come up? (*Little pause.*) I can't help being a mite perplexed, you see – not to have looked in on me once since I came back from hospital.

Anita I looked in on you every day for two months after you came back from hospital.

Jason Yes, that's true. Although looking in isn't quite – quite the right phrase. You fed me, you nursed me – for the first few weeks you virtually changed me. Like a baby.

Anita Actually, darling, not quite like a baby.

Jason No. I'm sorry. And I'm grateful. Of course I am. But it doesn't make sense, Neets. When I first came home I was already ill, wasn't I, I mean the state I was in – drunk from midday on, my stomach out to here, hands shaking, almost inert –

Anita Yes, and with that ghastly beard. You looked like a corrupt Father Christmas.

Jason Exactly. But you still came to me. Once you'd installed me in my flat – in fact, I thought that's why you installed me, so you'd be able to come to me whenever you felt like it. And you did. But now I'm better, fitter, fuller – of myself, my real self – than I've been for years and years – well, look at me, Neets, people in my neighbourhood refer to me as the Prof, and with good reason – I've got four articles coming out this month – in the *Times Literary Supplement*, the *New Statesmen and Nation*, *Encounter*, and the *Caribbean Review*. I'm becoming a literary journalist of some consequence, not to be sneezed at. I'm not to be sneezed at, Neets.

Anita I'm not sneezing at you, Japes. When have I sneezed at you?

Jason No. But then you never even look at me really, do you? Well, we're scarcely ever alone, you see to that, don't you? I spend far more time with Wendy. Christ, Neets, everything I've done – I went to Guyana because of you, and I stayed there because of you.

Anita (*after a pause*) Are you saying you became drunk and incompetent because of me?

Jason I'm saying that the whole of my life, everything, Neets, since the afternoon you stepped into this house has been because of you. Instead of you, because of you, Neets. (*Pause.*) And now I'm back, now I'm back – what have you turned me into? Uncle Japes. A small step up from having me around as a – as a pet, a dog, I suppose. I had a far better time when I was your corrupt Father Christmas – at least we – we played together.

Anita We fucked.

Jason Yes. But why then and not now?

Anita I thought you needed it. I thought you were dying. It was all I had to give and I thought it would be over soon.

Jason So I've sort of cheated, have I, by getting better?

Anita Well, we couldn't go on like that, could we, if we're both planning to live to a reasonable age? It would be – (*Thinks.*) – ridiculous. Much better all round if you're just Uncle Japes, household pet.

There is a little pause.

Have I hurt you?

Jason Well, if you have it's my own fault. I swore to myself I'd never, ever – as a matter of dignity . . . But dignity was never ever something that got between us, we've always been beneath it and above it.

Anita laughs.

Jason Ah. A remembered noise.

Anita looks at him, looks away again.
There is a pause.

Look me in the eye, Neets, go on, look me in the eye for once at last. And tell me you love me. Or tell me you don't love me. One or the other. Go on, have the guts, Neets, I deserve that much at least.

Anita Who's to say what you deserve – or me, what I deserve? And why does it have to be one or the other, love or not love, whether I look you in the eye or not? Look you in the eye – hah! (*Laughs.*) And perhaps I do like things as they are, yes, perhaps I do.

Jason But how could you? What are things as they are? You said yourself that you've got nothing to do except your church and your fretting over Wendy and being apart from Mychy – and me with nothing to do either except wait for you to come back to me, come back to life, both of us mouldering away while Mychy gets on with what Mychy has always got on with, living his life in the middle of us but apart – apart.

Anita So what do you want us to do, run away together?

Jason Yes. Yes, that's what I do want. Exactly that.

Anita Where to?

Jason I don't know, I don't care, anywhere you want.

Anita And Wendy?

Jason (*after a little pause*) She'll come with us. She should come with us.

Anita Should, why should?

Jason You know perfectly well why, Neets.

Anita And there we'd be, a perfect little family – intact. Oh, Japes – oh, poor, dear Japes. (*Begins to laugh.*) How can it be that you're not drunk? It must be Wendy's dope –

Jason goes to her, seizes her quite roughly by the shoulders.

Jason Look me in the eye. Go on, look me in the eye.

Anita looks at him.

Anita Well? (*Little pause.*) I'm looking. You see? Surely you can see. I'm too old and I can't be bothered any more.

Jason kisses her on the mouth, then with increasing passion. Anita resists with pushes and slaps even, Jason persists, quite brutally, Anita begins to respond, with increasing passion. They separate, heavy breathing, etc.

Jason You see? Now do you see? You're mine. I'm yours. That's where we belong. And that's all there is to it. (*Takes her in his arms again.*)

Anita (*responds, then pulls away*) Don't! Mychy might come in. Or Wendy.

Jason I don't care. Let them know, let them both know. It's time.

Sound of door opening.
Anita gets up, moves away, adjusting clothing.

Then come to me later. Come to me, Neets. Come to me.

Anita looks at him.

Anita Hi, darling! What are you up to? We're in here.

Michael (*enters*) So you are, I was just – just – I thought you'd both be in bed by now. (*as he slumps down*)

Anita No, we've been doing some old times – old times, is what we've been doing, while we've been waiting up for you.

Jason But what's the matter, Mychy, sloping about the streets like a burglar and rapist –

Anita He's depressed. Feels unworthy. His triumphs always make him feel unworthy.

Jason You gave a nice speech. Graceful.

Michael Grateful? That's how I sounded, is it? Grateful.

Anita He said graceful.

Michael Oh, yes. Graceful. Good. I think I need a drink. (*Gets up, goes to drinks table.*)

Jason Well – I think I'll be off.

Michael What, already?

Jason Yes, a bit tired. Oddly draining seeing someone one knows and loves – private faces in public places, might be nicer and brighter and all that but they're still a bit of a – (*Goes over to Anita, kisses her on cheek.*) See you, then.

Anita Yes, yes, see you.

Jason (*makes to go, turns*) But really, Mychy, you cut quite a figure – not just the speech that was graceful.

   Michael raises a hand.
    Jason goes.

Michael (*comes back, sits with drink*) Graceful figure. Graceful speech. On television.

Anita I think he did very well.

Michael Oh, he was graceful too, was he?

Anita Yes. Not easy for him, you know. You getting everything he wants and has never had even a sniff of – and then your being bitter about it, so he has to comfort you almost. I think he does bloody well, all round.

Michael And what about my daughter? She does well, too, I suppose.

Anita We don't know she didn't watch it with her chums.

Michael Yes we do. And it's appropriate. Deserved.

Anita What?

Michael That she didn't watch it. After all, I didn't do the thing I swore to myself I'd do. For her sake.

Anita And what was it you swore to yourself you'd do, for her sake?

Michael Behave badly, of course. Be resentful and rejecting. She would have appreciated that, seeing herself as my role model.

Anita You mean you actually thought of refusing it?

Michael Indeed. Indeed I did. In fact I'd worked out a speech telling them how squalid the whole business was, plays weren't in competition with each other, how dare a panel of any kind take it on itself to decide which play was best –

Anita It wasn't the best. It was the most promising. You got the most promising playwright award.

Michael Yes, well, it comes to the same thing. I was talking – would have been talking about the basic principle. About the people who make these decisions – best play, most promising play, best actor, best actress – the mere fact that they wanted to be on that sort of panel disqualified them from being on a panel like that – that's the sort of thing I wanted to say, the sort of thing one says when one isn't getting an award. Of any kind.

Anita Still, it's worth saying, isn't it? If you really do believe it.

Michael But I couldn't. They made it impossible. After all, they phoned up weeks in advance to tell me I'd got the bloody thing. I should have rejected it there and then, shouldn't I?

Anita Well, why didn't you?

Michael Because then they'd simply have given it to someone else and nobody would know I'd actually won. Of course they didn't tell me straight out that I'd only got the most promising, I assumed it was for the best – and then once I'd accepted it I was stuck with it – but I trust I looked as if I didn't want it with my – body language.

Anita Actually, darling, from your body language you looked as if you thought you didn't deserve it.

Michael And I didn't deserve it, because it was a bloody insult, that's what it was. Getting an award for promising to be anything, except a corpse, when you're my age –

I've got twelve novels to my name, two books of short stories, I've been nominated for a Booker three times, that's almost a record. I'm established, an established writer who for once chose to express himself through the theatre and suddenly I'm back to where I was two decades ago – promising.

Anita *Most* promising. Not just promising, most promising, and it's official. (*Points to award, laughs.*) So that's what's behind all this, I knew it.

Michael No, it's not what's behind all this. Everything's behind all this. My whole life is behind all this.

Anita Your whole life?

Michael Yes, the point of it. It suddenly doesn't look at all promising to me. Especially not the past. Not a promising past. Is my view.

Anita Really, what's missing from it, Mychy?

Michael Truth, honesty, honour.

Anita Really? (*Pours herself a drink.*)

Michael Fraudulence. A fraudulent past, a fraudulent life as so far lived. In fact I don't think I can go on. Why should I, eh? Tell me why.

Anita Well, you know, you are – whatever, Mychy, you're very much loved, so loved, so needed.

Michael Am I? That's good to hear. Certainly good to be told. (*Pause.*) I'm a coward, Neets. A fake and a coward. And you know it.

Anita No. No, I don't know it. How could I when you're not? And could never be. Why should you think you are, darling?

Michael Wendy knows, I can feel it. Unconsciously but somewhere in her system – as one's children always know. Or suspect. And Japes – well, of course – how could he not? And of course he'd die rather than express it, but sometimes I catch it in his eye, his brother's eye – not exactly as I catch it in Wendy's – less contempt, perhaps, but with less – less pity than I see in yours, my darling.

Anita (*extremely distressed*) Nobody feels contempt for you, Michael. How could they possibly? And if I feel pity for you it's only for your having me as your wife. For being what I am. For having done what I've done. But you, you've done everything, no man could have done more – you're generous and honourable to a fault, Mychy, and it's unbearable, unbearable to see you, hear you humble yourself – it's almost more than I deserve, and God knows, I deserve – I deserve –

Michael The truth? No, you don't deserve it – it's not fair on you, I know that, but in that you are my wife, poor soul, suffer me to face it, for my own sake. Will you? Please, darling?

Anita nods.

Here it is, then. As I understand it. (*Little pause.*) A consequential writer, an important writer, a major writer asks the questions. The same questions that the Greeks asked – Sophocles, Aeschylus – that Shakespeare asked, that Tolstoy – oh, every single bloody one of them! – why? That question, Neets – why? Why, why, why?

Anita Why what?

Michael Why are we, of course. Why?

Anita, after a pause, laughs.

What?

Anita Sorry, sorry, Mychy, it's just that – I mean –
I mean, you do ask that question, you do really, and you
ask lots of others too. To tell you the truth – truth –
(*Lets out a little laugh.*) – I've got a bit of a headache
and – and –

Michael I'll tell you what questions I ask, Neets, in
everything I've ever written including – (*Gestures towards
award, putting on a mincey voice.*) What does it feel like
to be betrayed by your wife? What does it feel like to
betray your wife? What does it feel like to be the wife
betrayed? Not why has God sent this mighty deluge down
upon us, but why am I pissing over my own shoes? At
least I could have pissed over somebody else's, made
a few enemies. I haven't got an enemy in the world,
Neets – think of it, a successful writer with no enemies.
Why I've never even had a bad review, not a seriously
bad one anyway, three or four mediocre ones – (*suddenly
remembering*) – five, yes, five mediocre ones, but no
seriously bad reviews, and no enemies – tells its own
story, doesn't it? When I'm dead and done with you
might look for me in the next century's footnotes – Cartt,
Michael – born nineteen thirty-eight, died nineteen ninety-
(*Gestures.*) – three, four – an affable but inconsequential
chronicler of middle-class domestic treacheries, particularly
noted for his fastidious syntax, his wry and dainty
cowardice – (*Laughs, swaying.*) – his fastidious, cowardly
and dainty syntax – oh, oh, to hell with it, the truth is –
yes, here's the truth – we're all pygmies, even the ones
who can't write, what does it matter which pygmy they
give an award to? They could do it alphabetically. Or
collectively. So to hell with it, to hell with it all –!

Anita Yes, to hell with it, because what seems pretty
pygmy to me is that whenever anything really – really
nice happens you get drunk and jeer and blame the
world – the world must be a really rotten place if it

allows you any little flourishing in it, so you do dirt on it, on everything in it, on everyone, on me and Japes and Wendy but most of all on yourself. Well, I don't want to hear it. Not any of it. Life is just as full of bad things as you say – most of all it's full of treachery and betrayal and – and death, too, just as you say, and we've got a daughter who – who – who knows whose she is, I mean who – who she is and what she is and how she got here or what she's up to, at this very minute, drugs or getting herself banged up and it may be our fault and it may be mine, or yours, or – or anybody's or quite simply hers – and so the question of why, why, why? – (*Gestures.*) And something, some little thing I want from you, I've wanted from you for months, no, going on years now, a year and a half actually, two years, *two* almost! – that matters, more than all the rest of it, I want to be fucked, I want you to fuck me again at last, you selfish shit, and it's because of your dinner jacket and your trophy, see? See?

Michael Now, you mean?

Anita This minute. This very minute.

Michael (*after a long pause*) Ah. (*Gets up, goes to her, kisses her. Takes her hand.*) Let's go, then.

Anita seems to allow herself to be led off, suddenly swerves towards his study, pulling him with her.

Anita Here. I want to do it here.

Michael Here? Why?

Anita Because I want us to defile it.

Michael You can't defile it. I've spent most of my life doing that. It's where I hope, dream, write, envy, hate, gloat, am frightened – it's a cesspit.

Anita (*savagely*) Well then, let's purify it. By loving each other in it. Let's bless your cesspit. Sanctify it. (*Goes into study.*)

Michael (*staying at door, looking in*) It's odd how you get drunker and drunker once you've stopped drinking.

Anita begins to undress.

Darling – let's face it, the bed's more comfortable.

Anita But it won't have the same meaning. No memories attached. Look – (*now in underwear*) – here she is. Your wife. In her panties and her bra. Just as you liked to see her. Preferably in a forbidden place. Years and years ago. (*taking his hand, pulling him into study*)

Michael (*resisting*) Oh, come on, darling. I'm sorry I was so – so disgusting and – mean-spirited and – but I need you in bed – I mean I –

Anita (*in doorway*) You mean you hope I'll fall asleep and then tomorrow you'll be back down here, and another night will have gone, another day be going – gone. And I'll have forgotten or be too embarrassed and shy to remind you, and whatever's going to happen to Wendy won't happen until the day after tomorrow and there'll be old Japes on the sofa the day after the day after tomorrow and tomorrow and tomorrow, here, look, I'm begging you – (*Gets down on her hands and knees.*) – please, husband, please. Give me a go. Unzip.

Michael (*fumbles with his flies*) Bugger, they're jammed again. Same thing happened at the awards, when I went for a pee, I had to go into a booth, take my trousers down – here, you try.

Anita Why?

Michael Well, it's stuck, I can't do it.

Anita But why not take your trousers down?

Michael Why not? If you don't mind the slightly lavatorial, um – (*Takes off his jacket, puts it over his chair, begins to work at pulling his trousers down, with slight difficulty because of the zip.*) They seem to have got tighter, or I've got fatter since – there, there – (*Gets them past his hip to his ankles.*) – well, there. (*Puts his hands on his hips, remembers his pants, pulls them down, puts his hands on his hips again.*) I'm not – well, as you can see, it's not exactly – must be the drink. (*Little pause.*) I need help, it seems.

Anita Let's see if we can get him to stand up. Like a man.

> *Busies herself with him. Michael makes slightly bogus sounds of excitement. Anita stops.*

Michael Sorry. Still a little shy. Not used to all this attention, I suppose.

> *Anita, still on hands and knees, gathers her clothes, goes to the sitting room. She lets out a baying sound, like a dog, gets up, puts on clothes, realises she's a shoe short, pours herself a drink, obviously comes to a decision, gulps it down, goes off.*
>   *Michael pulls up trousers, adjusts himself. As he does so, glances into study, comes out, carrying Anita's shoe. Turns off the light, closes the door firmly. Goes into sitting room, as if expecting to find Anita. Looks as if to go after her, pours himself a drink instead.*
>   *Anita comes in, wearing coat.*

You're going out, are you? (*handing her shoe*)

Anita Yes. (*putting shoe on*)

Michael Ah. Well, it's late, it might be risky, shall I come with you?

Anita Where to?

Michael I don't know. Where are you going?

Anita I don't know. To find a man who wants to fuck me, perhaps.

Michael Well, it still might be a bit risky. And I can always hold his coat. Or yours. (*Little pause.*) You're a bit unsteady, darling. We both are. Shouldn't we go to bed?

Anita No. No, I'm going out, and you're staying in. One of us has to be here for Wendy, make sure she comes back.

Michael How can my staying in make sure that she comes back? No, I think we should both stay in or I should come out with you. We can look for her if you want.

Anita Hah! Where? In what dump or dive, in what condition and in whose bed, eh? No, I'm going out, on my own, and you can stay here and worry about both of us, two for the price of one, if you want –

Sound of front door opening and closing.

Michael (*triumphantly*) Ah.

Jason (*enters*) Hi.

Michael Hi.

Anita (*laughs*) Hi.

There is a slight pause.

Jason (*nods*) Thought I'd better tell you – suddenly feel restless, rather restless, so I've decided to go away for a while. An impulse sort of thing. Didn't want to phone, in case you'd gone to bed.

Michael What, you mean you're off this minute?

Jason No, no, but tomorrow first thing. If I put it off it might be years before I stir.

Anita Stir?

Jason As in life. Stir into life. Have to take advantage of it while it still goes on – the stirring. The life, come to that.

Michael Anywhere specific?

Jason Mmmm?

Anita Are you going anywhere specific?

Jason Yes, well I thought – Antibes.

Michael (*who has gone to pour himself another drink*) So. Back to the Caribbean. Still got a hold on you, has it?

Anita Antibes. He said Antibes.

Michael Oh, sorry, I thought he said Ant – (*Gestures.*) – Antibes, of course, South of France, why there? Why Antibes, Japes?

Jason Well, from what I gather it's pretty – a pleasant climate, civilised atmosphere, interesting people –

Michael Interesting people? What interesting people?

Jason Well, I don't know yet, do I? Though isn't it the sort of place that writers, painters, phoneys – Graham Greene, doesn't he hang out there?

Michael So he does. Poor old Graham. Drinks like a fish. Bitter. Bitter and self-absorbed and drinks like a fish. (*pouring himself another drink*) Not really your type any more, Japes, I shouldn't think?

Jason Oh, I don't know. Anyway, can't hurt to take a look – not at Graham Greene, I mean, but the place – if I don't like it, I can always move on to somewhere else, in Italy perhaps, and if I don't like that, well – (*Laughs.*) – I can always come home. Back, I mean.

Anita No, you can't.

There is a pause.

If you have a strong impulse thing, a stirring, a life-stirring thing, you should follow it wherever it takes you. Go away, Japes. Go properly. Follow your star.

Michael But surely going to Antibes can't possibly count as going away properly, he can be there and back in a few hours. Why don't you think further, Japes, further than you've ever thought before, what about Japan?

Anita Yes, Japan! Go and stir in Japan, Japes. The land of sushi, geisha and – (*Gestures.*)

Michael Hiroshima. Hara kari. And kamikaze.

Anita Yes, hiro, hara and kami – (*Laughs.*)

Michael laughs.

Jason (*smiling*) Yes, well, I'll start off in Antibes, I think.

Anita is taking her coat off, with some difficulty.

Oh, were you going out then, Neets?

Anita I'm trying to take it off.

Jason Yes, but were you going to go out, did I stop you?

Anita It was an impulse – a stupid fucking stirring and impulse, now passed.

Jason If you still have the slightest inclination, I'd be glad to keep you company. For safety's sake.

Anita Thank you. What a couple of gallants you boys are, one or other of you always offering to be at my side, for safety's sake – well, I've had enough, enough, time to vanish. (*sinking onto sofa, lying back, closing eyes*) Go on, both of you, vanish please, and leave the world to darkness, and to me – isn't that one of your favourite lines, one of you, or is it both of you – leave the world to darkness – (*Subsides.*)

During this Michael and Jason have been eyeing each other.

Michael How's the leg?

Jason The leg?

Michael Yes, your leg, how is it these days? I haven't asked after it for a long time, have I? Too busy asking after all the other things – liver, heart, spleen, kidney – forgotten about the leg, how is it?

Jason It's itself, very much itself, thank you, Mychy.

Michael I suppose you don't even think about it any more. Just another part of you, really, it's become. No more crippled than the rest of you.

Jason Though I do sometimes find myself wondering what it would have been like if it had been the other way around.

Michael You mean if *you* had bounced *me* and *I'd* fallen off the diving board and buggered my leg, you mean?

Jason Actually, I did bounce you. And I did the falling off too. In fact you didn't do anything except keep your footing.

Michael Yes, well, either way, it wouldn't have made much difference.

Jason You'd have kept your footing on one good leg, and I'd have limped and hobbled around you on two, eh? Then that's all right, isn't it? Because it means there was never anything we could do about us.

Michael Hadn't you better go and pack for the morning, pack for Antibes?

Jason Oh, there's no rush, really – I haven't even booked a flight yet – I may go by train. And I do want to take a proper leave of our Wendy. Oh, by the way, Neets was saying just a moment ago that she's worried about our Wendy, and frankly, Mychy, so am I. I've done my little best to coax her towards maturity in the short time I've been back but now that I'm going –

Michael – we can send her on to you, in Antibes or wherever.

Jason No, I'm afraid not, Mychy, I'm too used to being a single man, I'm still not ready for that sort of responsibility yet. Best for you to try and see me as a drop-in, drop-out sort of uncle figure, really.

Michael Well, uncle figure, time for you to drop out.

Jason Mmm?

Michael Out of my life. All our lives. Get out, Japes. Go on. Fuck off. (*Throws his drink in Jason's face.*)

> *Jason, in panic at the alcohol, lets out a scream.*
> *Michael refills his glass.*
> *Anita has sat up.*
> *Michael throws contents towards Jason's face.*

Jason (*stumbles towards Michael, swinging stick*) You shit, you shit, you useless fucking shit, useless fucking writer, useless fucking husband, not even the fucking father, I'm the fucking father – (*Hitting and missing* *during this, collapses backwards on to the sofa, across Anita.*)

Michael (*picks up statuette, moves towards Jason*)
You're the fucking father, are you? You're the fucking father? (*Raises statuette, to deliver lethal blow.*) You're the fucking fucking fucking –

> *Anita screams.*
> *Michael freezes. He stares down at Jason and Anita. Pulls himself together. Gives a little laugh.*
> *Michael looks down at statuette, then walks across to shelf, puts it down carefully.*

I'm going to bed. (*Little pause.*) Night, Japes. Neets – um – Goodnight then.

Jason Night, Mychy.

> *Michael goes out.*
> *There is a pause.*

Anita I'd like to think that neither of you was the fucking father. Is. Is the fucking father. There are lots of other candidates. My money is on one of them. Preferably from Yorkshire. Yes, a Yorkshire lad, my money's on.

Jason Well, let's hope he turns up in a minute. Shares the load. I wish he hadn't thrown Scotch. I really wish he hadn't. (*rubbing his hand over his face*) The taste – (*Gets up, goes to the drinks table, pours himself a drink.*)

Anita Think before you drink.

> *Jason looks down at the drink, goes with it to the sofa, sits down beside Anita.*

He's quite right, you know. We were getting on reasonably well until you came back. You make such a mess – such a mess of everything, Japes.

Jason I suppose I'm what's called a force for life. (*Raises his glass, takes a gulp, shudders.*) Or a force for mess, depending on your point of view. Oh Christ!

Anita takes the glass from him, takes a gulp, hands it back to Jason. Jason takes a gulp, hands it back to Anita. Anita takes a mouthful, holds it in her mouth, looks at Jason.

You don't mean it.

Anita shrugs. Jason takes her in his arms, puts his mouth to hers, receives Scotch, swallows it, seizes her, kisses her. They begin to make love.
Lights.

SCENE THREE

Ten years later. The same. It is a mid-afternoon. The room is full of sunlight. There is the sound of Mozart coming from Michael's study and, just audible, the sound of typing. Wendy is sitting in a corner of the sofa. She is wearing a coat. She takes a cigarette out of her pocket, lights it, starts to smoke, stops herself, gets up, looks around the room, stubs out the cigarette. She is pregnant. She looks towards the study door, makes as if to go to it, goes instead to the window. Looks out. She feels her back. The sunlight is falling on her.
The music and the typing stop. There is a pause. Michael comes out of his study. He is carrying a glass. He goes to the drinks table, pours himself a drink. Smells cigarette. Sees the stub.
Becomes aware of Wendy, who has turned, is watching him, a presence in the sunlight.

Michael Neets!

Wendy (*comes towards him*) No, Dad. Not Neets. It's her daughter. (*There is a pause.*) What are you working on, then?

Michael My memoirs.

Wendy Your memoirs?

Michael Yes. (*Little pause.*) I'm having a go at my memoirs. Nothing too personal – really a sort of record of my time as I noticed it slipping towards me, around me, away from me. (*Sees glass in his hand.*) Would you like anything?

Wendy I'm not allowed anything I'd like.

Michael That must be hard. (*Drinks.*)

Wendy May I sit down? My back gets a bit stiff. (*Sits.*) You're well, then? You look quite well – just the same, really.

Michael Thank you. And are you well?

Wendy Yes, thank you. I'm pregnant.

Michael Oh. I thought you might be, but one can never be sure. It's embarrassing if one gets it wrong. (*Little pause.*) Is there a father?

Wendy No. I'm doing this on my own, Dad. It seems simpler.

Michael Ah. Well, if you need any help – financial help . . .

Wendy I knew I could count on your kindness. I remember one of your little lectures – kith, kin, kindness, in nature, remember? And how it had turned itself into a dead word. No sense of responsibility. No tribal significance.

Michael Well, that's frequently the way with words, the important ones, they come away from their stems, drift about like petals, into the breeze of this conversation and that – decorative and useless. You know that your mother's dead?

Wendy Yes. Where is she?

Michael Do you mean theologically or geographically?

Wendy I mean, where is she buried?

Michael Up the road. At St Mark's. The church she was so fond of. I was lucky to get her in, really. It was almost full. I believe they've closed it off, since.

Wendy What about Japes? Did you manage to get him in?

Michael Yes, I did.

Wendy Right beside her?

Michael Yes.

Wendy You gave them a joint funeral, then?

Michael Yes.

Wendy Is that usual?

Michael Not for me. But then it was a first, wasn't it? I wrote to you about it. I didn't know quite where to get hold of you so I sent it to the clinic – your last address, as known to me, hoping they'd send it on. It obviously didn't find you.

Wendy No. Well – it may have done but it wouldn't have mattered, I wasn't opening envelopes at that time. Particularly if they had familiar handwriting on them.

Michael Still, you found out about it.

Wendy From the newspapers. When I was in prison.

Michael Something to do with drugs, I suppose.

Wendy No, fraud actually. I got hold of someone's credit card – although you're right really, it's what they classify as a drugs-related crime when they make up those lists of drugs-related crimes. Anyway, everything I bought fraudulently, I sold for drugs. Did they do it on purpose?

Little pause.

Well, that's what they hinted in the newspapers. That they committed suicide in their Riviera love-nest or even that one of them had murdered the other and then –

Michael They were killed by fumes. From the garage below Japes's flat.

Wendy But they were found naked on top of the bed, weren't they?

Michael Exactly. And according to the French police, it's characteristic of suicides to present themselves respectably. In other words, properly dressed. *Comme il faut.* They'd also been drinking heavily. There were two empty bottles of Calvados by the bed. So they drank too much, fell asleep, and of course never noticed that the flat was full of fumes. They always tended to be a bit careless when they were together, having fun.

Wendy The last time I saw Japes, he wasn't drinking. He said he'd stopped for ever.

Michael Alcoholics do that regularly, don't they? Anyway, he chose to move to Antibes, a legendary place for drunks. Graham Greene, after all. I did warn him.

Wendy Was she living with Japes?

Michael Living with him?

Wendy Had she left you to live with him?

Michael Not to my knowledge.

Wendy Not to your knowledge!

Michael She came to my door and said she was going.

Wendy Your door?

Michael The door there. That door. My door. She knocked, as she always did. She came in. She was wearing a coat and carrying her overnight bag. She said she was going.

Wendy But she didn't say where?

Michael Every time she came to my door dressed for going and said she was going, I knew she was going to Japes.

Wendy So you expected her back then?

Michael Well, of course I expected her back. Just as I always expected her to go, I always expected her to come back.

Wendy And you didn't mind?

Michael On the contrary. I was pleased she had something to look forward to. Both coming and going.

Wendy What about their wills?

Michael Their wills?

Wendy Yes. Was I left anything?

Michael Your mother and I made an elementary will just after we got married, leaving everything to each other. We never got around to anything more complicated.

Wendy And Japes?

Michael He hadn't left a will. As I'm the next of kin what he had came to me.

Wendy What about Mum's personal stuff, did you keep any of it?

Michael I gave her clothes to Help the Aged.

Wendy Well – (*Little pause.*) – what about her other things, her jewellery and that?

Michael I sold it.

Wendy (*after a pause*) Did you, Dad? Sold it?

Michael I sold all Japes's books and personal things too. I gave all the money to that church your mother was so fond of. St Mark's. It seemed to me that's what she would have wanted. And Japes would have wanted what she would have wanted. (*Pause.*) I had to do everything by guesswork. After all, I had nobody to consult, did I? Perhaps I should have waited for you to be in touch, but then where were you? Dropped out, vanished, in another country or dead too, for all I knew.

Wendy No, it's all right, Dad. I understand how you came to do it, I really do. You wouldn't have wanted me around anyway. Far better for you to keep it between the three of you, as usual – that's what I thought when I read about it – that it was just the three of you, my dad, my uncle, and my mum, as usual, I didn't come into it, my proper place was in jail or wherever while all this moving and burying of their bodies and selling of their goods was going on, just like when I was little, and you were in there – (*pointing to his study*) – writing and writing away and Japes and Mum were being careless somewhere, probably in here even, eh Dad – having their fun and fucking and being fucked by each other.

Michael Yes, I suppose you have to use those words, don't you? It's the currency of your lot, isn't it?

Wendy My lot? (*Laughs.*) The proper words for it matter, Dad. To me, anyway. To my lot. Because that's what they did, Dad, isn't it, they fucked each other?

Michael Your mother and my brother were frequently in love with each other. They loved each other always.

Wendy And you knew. Always knew that they – 'loved' each other. And were frequently 'in love' with each other.

Michael I understood it, now and then.

Wendy And you didn't mind?

Michael Now and then.

Wendy Well, what about now, as opposed to now and then? Eh, Dad? What do you feel now?

Michael A sense of completeness. It's run its course, the story. It's over. (*Little pause.*) I talk to them.

Wendy As a couple? Or individually? And what about?

There is a pause.

Oh, sorry, Dad. I shouldn't pry, should I, as it's so sacred. But would you mind telling me so that this one – (*Pats womb.*) – can know which one's the grandfather and which one's the great-uncle?

Michael I don't know. None of us ever knew for sure.

Wendy And you don't care, do you? What does that sort of thing matter to you lot from the sodding sixties? With your love, love, love and your freedom and flowers and all belonging to each other so what does it matter where the children came from or who they belong to, as long as they're born in love, love, love and the joys of sex? Well, it matters to me, Dad. I don't give a fuck about your lot or my lot, but I give a fuck about this one, and our life together, I want to know whether you're my uncle or my father, Dad.

Michael I was your father, Wendy, in every important respect. In every practical respect. My name was on your birth certificate. And on every cheque that was needed for your provision, and for every institution you attended, from your nursery school to your drugs clinic. Japes was only there for you as an uncle, to give you presents and treats.

Wendy He was also my best friend. I used to think of him as the only friend I ever had.

Michael Then he's unlikely to be your father, isn't he? Why should you want him to be?

Wendy I'm not saying I want him to be. I'm saying I intend to find out. I'm a long way from the nursery school and the clinic now, Dad. I know what's going on around me, things like DNA, for instance. I'm sure you know all about it, too. So you see, Dad, here we are and we want our dues.

Michael (*pause*) As you seem to feel a need for Japes to be your father I'm very happy to let you have him. More than happy.

Wendy Good. Thank you, Dad. Because if Japes is my father, you're not his next of kin. I am. And everything you got from him belongs to me. Including half this house.

Michael Half the house? So that's what you've come for, is it, half the house?

Wendy No, not for half of it. All of it. This is the only home I've known, and I never got to live a life in it. Our home, it's going to be. (*Little pause.*) It's up to you, Dad.

(*Little pause.*) I've already got myself a shrink. We're delving into my past and helping me remember things, we've already found out that there was more than just neglect when I was a child, there was trauma and abuse. There was a bedtime bogeyman. One of you was my bedtime bogeyman.

Michael And will you have me DNA-tested for that?

Wendy My shrink says the way we're working, we'll get to you in the end.

Michael To me.

Wendy To one of you.

Michael I see. And what did this bogeyman get up to, may I ask?

Wendy Well, as he was a bedtime bogeyman, Dad, it's obvious the kind of thing he got up to, isn't it?

Michael On the occasions when I put you to bed I read you a Janet and John story. Surely you remember Janet and John? This is Janet. This is John. Hello, Janet. Hello, John. There was one about wellington boots. It was raining but John wouldn't wear his wellington boots. His mother said, 'Wear your wellington boots, John, or your feet will get wet.' His sister Janet said, 'Wear your wellington boots, John, or your feet will get wet.' But John wouldn't wear his wellington boots. 'Silly old wellington boots,' said John. 'I shan't wear them!' Then they all went out into the rain, and soon John said, 'Oh, my feet are wet!' 'I told you so,' said his mother. 'I told you so,' said his sister Janet. So they went home and John put on his wellington boots. Then they went back out into the rain. 'Good old wellington boots,' said John, as he jumped up and down in the puddles. 'Good old wellington boots!'

Wendy (*shakes her head*) Pity I didn't remember it though, years ago. It might have stopped me from getting my feet wet, eh, Dad? No, all I can remember is the bogeyman, his voice saying, 'I am your bogeyman,' and chasing me around and around, from corner to corner, and when I got past him and hid in bed he'd come up the stairs, clumping up, one foot clumping after another foot clumping, with gaps in between, long gaps, short gaps, saying over and over again, 'I am your bogeyman, the bogeyman has got you,' and I'd be quivering with terror and laughter, both, I'd feel him above me, and I'd feel him bend down, he'd wait. And then – wait. And then he'd whisper, 'Your bogeyman has got you,' and he'd rip the covers right off, and scoop me in his arms. (*Little pause.*) And then when he'd finished with me he'd tuck me in and kiss me on the forehead, and I'd lie there until Mum came in. She'd sit on my bed and sing to me, 'Golden slumbers seal your eyes' – (*Sings first few lines.*) – and kiss me on the forehead and go off to bed, and then I'd hear your voices coming up, the two of you, laughing and talking and arguing and after a time I couldn't tell you apart, which was speaking and which was laughing and which was shouting, sometimes you'd both be doing it together as if there was just one of you doing it all by yourself, like a medieval devil. So perhaps that was it, really. You were both my bogeyman, turn and turn about.

Michael It's all a lie – a disgusting lie – and you know it.

Wendy Well, I don't think that's what my shrink thinks.

There is a little pause.

Michael There isn't even a shrink, is there? You're just making him up.

Wendy I'm not making her up. I just haven't got around to choosing her yet. But it won't be a problem, there'll

be hundreds and hundreds of them out there just waiting for the chance. And then we can leave it to the court to sort out, though I expect when it comes to it, if Japes turns out to be my real dad, I'd like you to be the bogeyman, Dad, as I'll already have got everything he's got, so it's best that you're up for the bogeyman damages.
I mean, you're the survivor, aren't you, poor old Dad!

Michael That you should come back like this and break into my life, my life – with your disgusting lies and blackmail and talk of dues, your dues, your dues! (*Breaks off, stares at her, in bewilderment, then almost to himself.*) It's not been like this. Not for other generations. Not in my understanding. We didn't start the world, our lot. We didn't come out of nowhere and just – just start you lot off. We were begot, just like you. We were just three people, struggling with ourselves, with each other, in our time. Don't you understand? Don't you understand that?

Wendy Your time, yes, well, you had a responsibility to the time that was coming. Coming out of your time. (*Goes over to him.*) Here, Dad. (*Takes his hand, puts it on her womb.*) There. You see. Can you feel her?

Michael No. (*Little pause.*) Yes. (*Little pause.*) Yes. I can.

Lights.

THE HOLY TERROR

Melon Revised

The Holy Terror was first broadcast on BBC Radio Three in October 1989. The cast included:

Mark Melon James Laurenson
Gladstone Robin Bailey
Samantha Susie Brann
Michael Sylvester Morand
Jacob Brian Miller
Rupert Struan Rodger
Graeme Joe Dunlop
Josh Melon Samuel West
Gladys Powers Joan Walker
Kate Melon Marcia King
Shrink Geoffrey Whitehead

The Holy Terror was first performed on stage at the Temple of Arts Theatre, Tucson, Arizona, on 15 February 1991. The cast was as follows:

Mark Melon Daniel Gerroll
Gladstone George Hall
Samantha Tracy Sallows
Michael Anthony Fusco
Jacob Anthony Fusco
Rupert Anthony Fusco
Graeme Anthony Fusco
Josh Melon Noel Derecki
Gladys Powers Julie Boyd
Kate Melon Rebecca Nelson

Shrink 1 George Hall
Shrink 2 George Hall

Director Simon Gray
Set Design David Jenkins
Costume Design David Murin
Lighting Dennis Parichy
Sound Brian Jerome Peterson
Production Stage Manager Cheryl Mintz

The Holy Terror was revived by the Ambassador Theatre Group and Laurence Boswell Productions, opening at the Theatre Royal, Brighton, on 4 February 2004. The cast was as follows:

Mark Melon Simon Callow
Kate Melon Geraldine Alexander
Josh Melon Matt Canavan
Gladstone/Shrink Robin Soans
Michael/Jacob/Rupert/Graeme Tom Beard
Gladys Power Beverley Klein
Samantha Eggerley Lydia Fox

Director Laurence Boswell
Designer Es Devlin
Lighting Designer Adam Silverman
Sound Designer Fergus O'Hare
Composer Simon Bass

Characters

Mark Melon

Gladstone

Samantha

Michael

Jacob

Rupert

Graeme

Josh Melon

Gladys Powers

Kate Melon

Shrink 1

Shrink 2

The action of the play takes place in the
Cheltenham Women's Institute, where Mark Melon
is giving a talk; and in his memory, as he gives it.
Two chairs face each other downstage; behind them
is a window in which, from time to time,
characters appear and disappear.

Act One

Melon Ms, um, chairperson, ladies and – well, ladies, eh? First I am under instruction to tell you not to worry. When your delightful Mrs Macdonald told me of the tradition of your tea break, a tradition far more honoured in the observing than in the breach, as Mrs Macdonald wittily put it, I decided to play absolutely safe by bringing along this rather natty little alarm clock – a recent birthday present from someone – someone very dear to me – and I've set it to go off at four-fifteen precisely. So don't be alarmed by the alarm, eh, it's rather loud and piercing, and rush for the exits thinking there's a fire or some such. Rush to the exits by all means, but only for your tea and sandwiches. There. We've got almost the most important thing out of the way, haven't we? But I hope that the rest of what I say won't be just a way of filling time until the tea and sandwiches, oh, and cakes, too, I know, as Mrs Macdonald allowed me a little peep at them on the way in, what a scrumptious selection – but even so, with those in prospect, I hope I'll be able to say something interesting about my life and times as a publisher. A little warning here, though, ladies. I'm not one for formal addresses carefully structured and skilfully organised and meticulously rehearsed. All I've got to keep me on the straight and narrow, so to speak, are a few notes on a few cards, so that when I'm in danger of getting lost, or even worse, losing you, I can furnish myself with a little signpost and so point my nose back towards you, here in Chichester. Cheltenham, that is. So sorry, ladies. If I sometimes confuse them in my mind, it's only because

they sound the same, and they share a tranquillity, a
charm, a peacefulness that is balm to the turbulent soul –
so indeed I felt this morning, when I got off the train and
treated myself to a little stroll along the leafy avenues.
Such a relief from the broil and moil, the lunacy –

Kate appears in the window right.

– um, chaos (*faltering, upset*) of London life. As Kate,
my wife, Kate, always used to say . . .

Kate disappears from the window.

Time for a card methinks, eh? But where are they? I had
them here. In my hand. I know I did. Ah yes. Here we
are. Card number one. 'Say sorry.' Say sorry? But what
for? I haven't said anything to say sorry for yet, have I?
Oh, it must be to apologise in advance for some of the
things I might suddenly find myself saying. Yes. Indeed.
That's it – it must be. Because I've discovered from recent
experience that one of the dangers of a freewheeling style
is that certain matters tend to bob up by association so
to speak, that may be quite relevant – so I'm not talking
about getting lost here – quite relevant, in fact of the
utmost relevance but nevertheless be a trifle – a trifle
unexpected. By being rather personal. So if I should find
myself suddenly describing myself as behaving like a
Hashemite widow, as I've been known to do when
speaking publicly – known to describe myself, I mean,
not actually behave like a Hashemite widow – good
heavens, I hope not, no, no, that sort of thing is all very
much in the past. I'm not actually sure, now that I've
spoken the words, that I know what a Hashemite is, by
the way. Do any of you ladies know what a Hashemite
is? Oh, well, never mind. I'm sure we can all imagine
how his widow would behave, can't we? Gosh, I feel
comfortable! Here in this room with so many kind and

interested ladies – at least you look interested, thank you
for that – there was a time, you know, and not so long
ago either, when I would have laughed out loud at the
thought of standing here in front of you today. Yes,
I would not only have thrown an invitation to address
the Chichester – Cheltenham Women's Institute straight
into the waste-paper basket, but I'd have made a bawdy
joke or two into the bargain. You can guess the sort
of thing. Well, I can tell you, ladies, not any more.
Things have changed. It's not my habit these days to
make jokes about women, or indeed about sex. There
seems to me nothing funny to be found in either, so
never fear, ladies, you won't be getting any bawdiness
from me! But now you're probably saying to yourself,
'Oh, I do wish the silly fellow would stop telling us
what he's not going to tell us, and just get on with it
and tell us what he is going to tell us.' And if you're not,
it's only because you're too kind and patient. So why
don't I just leap in and – and – now where did I intend
to start? Oh yes. 'Conquering all before me.' Perhaps
I shouldn't have read that out, it does sound so
immodest, doesn't it? But the truth is, it's the truth.
I began my career in publishing with a company I'm sure
you'll all have heard of, called Dominicus, Dominicus
Publishing, and – I began as an assistant editor, then
I became an editor, and then I became a senior editor
and was quite successful as a senior editor and then I
became a managing editor and – and so I conquered all
before me.

Gladstone enters to sit on chair, left.

Well, no – no, those weren't my great days, my halcyon
days, no, they came later when I took over Haylife and
Gladstone. (*to Gladstone*) Well, Edward, you play your
cards and I'll play mine.

Gladstone Well, as I'm sure you understand, Mark, what we want above all is to maintain our reputation as a great publishing house with great traditions.

Melon Presumably you also wish to remain solvent.

Gladstone Our economic difficulties won't, I hope, lead us into pursuing current trends and fads –

Melon In other words, you'd prefer not to move with the times.

Gladstone With the times, yes. Certainly with the times. But the values that made us what we are –

Melon Were.

Gladstone Mmmm?

Melon What you were, Edward. You aren't any longer what you were. What you are is nearly bankrupt. Or you wouldn't have sent for me, would you?

Gladstone We have the greatest respect for what you've done at Dominicus Publishing. Who were, though of course in a less distinguished way, having a less distinguished list –

Melon – in less of a pickle than you are.

Gladstone Some of our finest literary adornments are still alive and kicking.

Melon Cut the crap, Edward. You're going to go under in two years – possibly eighteen months – unless you do something very quickly. And the quickest thing you can do is to take me on as a full partner. In order to do that, you have to give me editorial control. I shan't mind the board meeting regularly to hear, approve and endorse my decisions, as long as it doesn't take up too much of my time.

Gladstone My only wish, you know, speaking personally, is to relinquish the reins, retire completely to my little attic and get on with collating my memoirs. You haven't any idea what I've got up there! Letters from Ezra Pound, Tom Eliot, even Yeats – yes, even Yeats –

Melon I'd like to begin recruiting immediately. My own editors. Right down to secretaries and so forth.

Gladstone What?

Melon Editors.

Gladstone Editors. Oh, don't worry about editors, Mark, we've got some very fine ones, as I'm sure you know. With your experience –

Melon They've got to go, Edward!

Gladstone Go? Go where?

Melon Go where they like once I've fired them.

Gladstone Fired them? But – I can't be party – not after all these years –

Melon You're not party to anything, Edward. If I'm running the show I'll do all the important work, including the dirty work. Now tell me about your personal secretary.

Gladstone My personal secretary?

Melon Yes. Tell me about her.

Gladstone That's my dear Mrs Muncie. She's been with us – oh, for many, many years. An absolutely devoted, conscientious, self-sacrificing . . . a treasure, really. A complete treasure. I couldn't manage without her.

Melon Well, you'll have to, won't you, Edward? Once you've relinquished the reins you won't be needing a personal secretary any more – your treasure will be coming over to me – but don't worry, only for a few minutes, Edward. Then she'll be on her bike.

Gladstone Her bike?

Melon Unless, of course, you're prepared to pay for her out of your own pocket. Then you can keep her on. Well, Edward. What do I say to Muncie? On her bike or out of your pocket?

Gladstone Oh, my poor Charlotte, my poor, poor Charlotte. Tell her.

Melon Oh, what a brute! Oh, what a beast! Oh, what a brute and a beast to ride roughshod over that dignified old gentleman, that's what you're thinking, aren't you, ladies? But – and yes, there's a but! Funny how there's always a but, isn't there? Whether you want to kiss it or kick it, the but's always there. Excuse my little play on words, turning the conjunction but into the part of the body butt, which is of course an Americanism for – for – I think it's the Americans who are always – urn – kissing or – um – kicking their – their – but – but – um, the truth is I can't – I can't quite – (*Looks at his cards in panic, then remembers.*) Oh, yes! That's it! The truth. The truth about Edward Ewart Gladstone. Yes, you were quite right, ladies, quite right in thinking of him as an old bore and an old nuisance, that's how I've always thought of him myself, but where you're wrong – absolutely wrong! is in thinking that he's also an old fool. (*standing behind him, caressing him*) He may not have heard a word I said, but he knew he was getting exactly what he wanted. Someone who knew not only whom to fire, which was virtually everybody, but how, which was quickly. From top to bottom I went – senior editors, editors, assistant editors, junior editors, right down to the last clucking, maternal antique of a Mrs Muncie.

'Shoots' Mrs Muncie as Gladstone exits.

Right, Miss Eggerley, let's see what you can do. On your marks – get set – go!

Samantha enters to right of centre.

Dear Mr Sudsbury comma re my plan to move our distribution centre from Hull to Watford stop It is important that you do everything to facilitate this highly cost-effective decision stop Further excuse for delay will not be accepted stop Therefore kindly exclude from future professional correspondence all references to the difficulties of your domestic situation stop Your problems with your wife are not the concern of your employers stop Furthermore your visits with her to the police station, social worker, psychiatric wards etcetera must be confined to your leisure hours stop Sincerely Mark Melon. Now read it back to me.

Samantha Dear Mr Sudsbury, re my plan to move our distribution centre from Hull to Watford. It is important that you do everything to facilitate –

Melon Spell facilitate.

Samantha F-a-c-i-l-i-t-a-t-e.

Melon Well, Miss Eggerley, you've learnt two things from that letter, haven't you? That I demand speed and efficiency and I don't put up with any nonsense. Do you still want to work for me?

Samantha Yes.

Melon Why?

Samantha Well – because – because I want to be in publishing, Mr Melon.

Melon Why?

Samantha Well, I've always been interested in books.

Melon Books?

Samantha Well – literature. English literature. I'm working for my O levels now. I left school early, you see. And then I decided to go back. In the evenings.

Melon You're planning to go to university?

Samantha Oh no.

Melon Not ambitious then?

Samantha Well – yes. But I like reading, you see. Studying helps me read. Makes me. I don't care whether I pass the exams, really.

Melon You're ambitious. You want to go to university. Until you do you'd like to knock about in publishing. But we're just something on your way to somewhere else. Which means we'd have to replace you about the time we'd got you properly trained and useful. Right?

Samantha It's not altogether like that. Really.

Melon No. Well, I'm sorry to hear that, Miss Eggerley. Because I want everybody here to be ambitious about something. As far as I'm concerned it's the only completely necessary qualification.

Samantha I'd like to work here very much. I'd do my best. I really do want to be in an atmosphere of books –

Melon So you keep saying. But now I come to think of it publishers aren't likely to provide it. At least this publisher. What I want here is an atmosphere of success, with no time wasted on idle reading and other forms of self-abuse. That's meant to be a joke, Miss Eggerley. With a germ of truth in it, of course. If you come to work here you'll have to get used to my jokes, and learn how to respond to them. They're not very good jokes, sometimes almost impossible to identify as jokes, but I generally help people to detect them by laughing at them myself. Rather loudly. Sometimes I even slap my knee. Is that your letter of application, Miss Eggerley?

Samantha Yes, yes it is.

Melon I see that your first name is Samantha, Miss Eggerley. What do your friends call you? Sam or Sammy?

Samantha Well, Samantha, actually.

Melon Pity, I'd have put my money on Sammy. I've always wanted to know a girl called Sammy. One last thing, Miss Eggerley. If you come to work here, I don't want any office romances or girlish gossip in the lavatories. Or flouncing about or tears or pouting because you get the occasional sharp word from me. You'll be here to do a job, and if you don't do it with charm and obedience you'll be out on your bum in no time, is that understood?

Samantha I've changed my mind, Mr Melon. I don't want the job after all.

Melon Why not?

Samantha I don't like the way you just spoke to me.

Melon In that case I shall have to try not to do it again, shan't I? You're hired as from Monday.

Samantha exits. Stands framed in window, right.

Well, there you – there you – But where was I? Why was I . . . with Sammy – hiring her, yes, that was it, wasn't it, ladies, hiring her at the very bottom. And then I – I think I need a little help again, eh. 'Say sorry.'

Samantha exits from window.

No no, we've had that – and that – and card number three we're up to, aren't we? 'Don't boast.' Oh no, that's a general note to myself – I do hope I haven't, if I have, my apologies, ladies. No boasting from this time forth – yes, here we are, card number three, 'My genius for unexpected recruiting at the higher levels, too, start with Ruff.' Ruff? Michael Ruff. 'Quote old publisher's axiom made up by self. Those that can, write. Those that can't, edit!'

Michael has entered – Melon speaks to him.

Michael.

Michael Mark!

Melon Is it confirmed that you're pregnant? No, I mean that you are going to have a baby, the two of you? That Melissa's pregnant, in other words? Is it confirmed, Michael?

Michael Yes, it is confirmed, Mark. She's pregnant.

Melon Congratulations.

Michael Thank you.

Melon What are you going to call it?

Michael We thought we'd call it Jocasta if it's a girl.

Melon Jocasta?

Michael Yes. And Marcus if it's a boy. Not exactly after you. But somewhere behind you, Mark, with you in mind.

Melon What do you intend to do about accommodation? Battle it out in that one room, the three of you?

Michael Well, we can't really do that, of course, not the three of us in the one small room, it isn't big enough for the two of us –

Melon Haylife and Gladstone need an editor. Responsible mainly for poetry and fiction. We can pay ten thousand a year. I can wangle you three mornings off a week for your writing. Well, what do you say, Michael?

Michael Well, it's generous, very generous of you, Mark – you're always such a good friend, unexpectedly good if I may – when it really counts – but I don't think – you see, I don't think – I'd have to talk it over with Melissa of course but she's already worried that I'm going to abandon what she calls my art – and she feels strongly that –

Melon (*interrupting*) I'm not asking you to join just any publishing company, Michael, but to join Haylife and Gladstone. It has the most distinguished poetry and fiction fist in the country. Just think of the great names.

Michael I know. I know. Yeats, Eliot, Pound –

Melon Your responsibility would be to add to them. And to add yourself to them.

Michael So you'd be publishing me, then?

Melon Well, Haylife and Gladstone would be. In other words, I hope you'd be publishing yourself.

Michael I see.

Melon We'd want first refusal on anything you wrote – you'd have to give us that, of course, in return for the time off we'd be giving you to write it in. Now tell me about your play – how far have you gone with it? When can you take a look at it as our editor?

Michael Well, I've only roughed in a few scenes as yet. But it's essentially going to be a comedy of contemporary manners. Infidelity, greed, political corruption. Set in a country house. But written in heroic couplets.

Melon Heroic couplets?

Michael Yes, heroic couplets. Oh, I know it isn't a fashionable form at the moment, but, then, no form is fashionable until somebody sets the fashion.

Melon (*turning to audience/ladies*) Heroic couplets, need I say more? I bet most of you ladies have forgotten what they are, think they're famous twins from the age of chivalry or something, eh? It's such a long time since I've come across them that I'm not sure I can quote any to give you a feel, but the first line goes tee-tum tee-tum tee-tum tee-tum tee-tum, the last tee-tum being a word you can rhyme with easily, and the second line goes tee-tum tee-tum tee-tum tee-tum tee-tum, the last tee-tum rhyming with the word you can rhyme easily with from the first line. Got it, ladies? So what old Michael would need for a play written in heroic couplets would be a heroic audience, eh? Actually, it would be like being at a tennis match, except that instead of your head going back and forth, it would go up and down – tee-tum tee-tum tee-tum – so needless to say, ladies, I'd as soon publish Melissa's pregnancy diary, with all medical notes attached, than Michael's play. Not that I had to worry about that. After all, old Michael has too much integrity as an editor ever to accept anything written by himself as an author. In fact, that was one of the minor reasons for employing him, to make sure that nothing of his was ever published. Now I'm sure you know as well as I do, ladies, and if you don't, your husbands will have told you, that all the great achievements, in publishing, just as in poetry, music, architecture, plumbing, require one, luck, two, hard work, three, dedication, four, cunning, five, cunning and six cunning. Right up to ten, cunning.

Gladstone (*entering*) Mark, a word if you please . . .

Michael (*entering*) Hello, Edward.

Gladstone Oh, hello, young man, hello.

Michael I've been meaning to ask – how are your memoirs coming along? I just happen to have glanced into the attic –

Gladstone What?

Michael Glanced into the attic.

Gladstone Danced into the attic?

Michael No. Glanced into the attic. I've been thinking – would you like me to help you sort through –

Gladstone Excuse me. Do excuse me, please. I'm frightfully busy. I'll leave you to Mark –

Michael Well, if you do need any help –

Gladstone exits.

Have you noticed that he always leaves the room the moment I come in?

Melon Yes, and I'm very grateful. He's a dear old dog, but he does rather use up valuable time.

Michael Perhaps. But he never leaves the room when other people come in, in fact they usually complain that they can't get him out. And this morning, the way he kept scowling at me during the board meeting. I just can't imagine what I said!

Melon You really mustn't get paranoid, Michael. The truth is he admires you enormously, but he finds your intellect rather formidable.

Michael Oh, I see.

Melon You make him a bit nervous. And he wasn't
scowling at you this morning. He was thinking very
seriously about your proposal for sex manuals. He was
just telling me he believes it could be a winner. As so do I.

Michael My – my proposal! But that was a joke.

Melon A joke?

Michael Yes. I said that if we go on doing some of the
things on our present list, we'd end up putting out sex-
instruction manuals –

Melon Really? Well, I wouldn't tell Edward that. It might
make him feel a bit of a fool.

Michael But surely, Mark, you realised it was a joke?

Melon To tell you the truth, Michael, I thought it was
such a humdinger of an idea that I didn't care whether it
came in joke form or not.

Michael But you're not seriously thinking – you're not
seriously thinking that Haylife and Gladstone of all
people should put out sex-instruction manuals?

Melon Why not? Haylife and Gladstone have an
obligation to take care of ordinary folk, too, Michael.
And what group in our society – many of them very
ordinary folk indeed – gets least attention when it comes
to sexual matters? The lonely, the neurotically shy, the
desperate bachelors and spinsters.

Michael Well, granted, but – but –

Melon So, following your idea through, we won't go in
for any old sex manuals, but thorough, well-written,
compassionately unembarrassed ones. We'd be using the

name of Haylife and Gladstone to a really important social end. Just as you've always wanted, Michael.

Michael Well – I must remember to try out a few more jokes at board meetings, eh?

Melon Absolutely. Keep them coming. I'd like you to take charge of it, Michael. To guarantee good taste. We'll call it *Masturbation without Shame*. Start with a prospectus. Circulate it with your name on it so that people know we're serious. And for God's sake make sure Edward gets a copy.

Michael Right. Right. *Masturbation without Shame*. And a copy for Edward. I'll start right away. And it'll make an exciting change from writing all those letters of rejection. (*Exits.*)

Gladstone (*entering*) Mark, a word, if you please, about that young man you just brought in as poetry and fiction editor.

Melon If you mean Michael, Edward, he's been with us for nearly five years.

Gladstone What?

Melon He's been with us *five years*, Edward!

Gladstone Really? That long! Well, it's evident he's still very raw to our ways. Naturally we all understand he wants to cut a dash, but nevertheless I have to tell you, Mark, that I find his manners at our editorial boards quite alarming. Must he debate quite so ferociously, while remaining completely inaudible? You will please correct me on this, Mark, but the only thing of his I heard distinctly, or distinctly thought I heard this morning, was his suggestion that we should launch sex-instruction manuals. You know I've always endorsed everything you've committed us to, but then your common sense and energy are always accompanied by an innate good taste, Mark –

Melon I hope and believe that that's not true, Edward.

Gladstone Not at all. You deserve every tribute. But it's quite clear that that young man has yet to come to terms with what our house has always represented, and I am dismayed, yes I admit *dismayed,* that it should even pass through his mind that we should give our imprimatur to such a project.

Melon It's just that he passionately believes we should think less about literature and more about the needs of everyday folk.

Gladstone What?

Melon Needs. Of everyday folk.

Gladstone A joke! A joke you say! But surely – surely he doesn't think our monthly board meetings – conducted at the famous long table, the table that Ezra Pound himself helped us to choose – are occasions for frivolity and obscenity?

Melon I don't know what else they're occasions for.

Gladstone Exactly. Exactly. And I'll leave you to put him in his place. (*Exits.*)

Michael (*entering*) Mark, Mark, I forgot to mention – one of my reject author's transcripts has gone missing. I was sure it was on my desk yesterday evening. An absolutely ghastly novel by a woman called Gladys something. Gladys Powers. All about what she calls the self-bondage tendencies of women. You can imagine the sort of thing. I read some of it out to Melissa. It made her absolutely livid. So I was wondering if it had come your way –

Melon How is Melissa?

Michael Oh . . . well . . . you know . . . dreadfully worried about Marcus. As I am. They're threatening to expel him from his nursery school. He's been beating up the other children, you see. The little girls, to be precise. Just runs up to them and boots away at them until the teachers drag him off.

Melon Sounds perfectly natural to me.

Michael Yes, but the trouble is . . .

Melon Good God, I've got an author due any moment!

Michael Oh, then I'd better clear off. I'll start in on *Masturbation without Shame* right away.

As Michael starts to exit Melon calls out.

Melon Oh, Michael, throw in a few diagrams, I think.

Michael Right, Mark, I'll do that. Diagrams. Right. Thank *you*. (*Exits.*)

Melon See, ladies, how I turned a potentially lethal situation into an office sport and a profit-making one? Furthermore, I had a gift for detecting talent in some of the most unexpected people. No one could accuse me of wanting to stamp out the creative urge. On the contrary. I looked for potential. I encouraged it. I had a feeling for it – a great feeling for it. Take what I still regard as my greatest coup – Jacob Isaacson, my little friend Jacob, so reticent, so remote, so full of pain and doubt . . .

Jacob has entered and sat in chair, left. Melon turns and speaks to Jacob.

Jacob. Did you bring it with you?

Jacob Bring what?

Melon Your diary of your trip to Israel. What it's really like to live on a kibbutz. What I want from you is kibbutz life as observed by a sensitive, Cambridge-educated, middle-class Jew. I hope you haven't made it sound like summer camp with the fear of death thrown in.

Jacob I'm afraid I didn't stay on a kibbutz, Mark. As a matter of fact, I didn't even go to Israel.

Melon What? Where have you been these last few months, then?

Jacob Here, in London, in the East End. Working in my uncle's practice. I've been desperately busy – that's why I haven't been in touch.

Melon What the hell do you want to go down to the East End for, surely you can do better than that? Anyway, I thought you wanted to be a psychiatrist –

Jacob Yes, well, you see, I have an idea that a lot of mental illness could be detected much earlier. And an ordinary practice in the East End might be just the place to do it. A lot of those patients who come in demanding nose-drops are really looking for a way of talking about their nightmares, their erratic behaviour – I want the truth of other lives. Now that I've decided to live out the truth of my own life. You see, Mark – you see – I'm a homosexual. And I've decided to come out of the cupboard at last.

Melon Now, Jake, do try to get our idioms right. We keep our skeletons in the cupboard, and our queens in the closet.

Jacob You're not surprised then?

Melon Oh come on, Jake, the only thing I don't under-stand is why you've pussy-footed around your own inclinations for so long. Being homosexual has been legal for years now. Not only legal, but in some quarters mandatory. Try buying a theatre ticket, for instance – That's our book!

Jacob What?

Melon Well, think about it, Jake. What it's like for a sensitive, Cambridge-educated Jewish queer to work with the shop-soiled psyches and moral disorders you're bound to come across down there in the East End. That's our diary! And that's our title – *The Shop-Soiled Psyche*.

Jacob *The Shop-Soiled Psyche*. Oh. Well, really, Mark, I couldn't do that, you know. I mean, let people talk to me thinking I was their friend and confidant, and then afterwards go back and write them up –

Melon Oh, don't write them up, Jake. Far too inaccurate. Use a concealed tape-recorder.

Jacob Really, Mark!

Melon A joke, Jake, a joke! (*to audience/ladies*) Oh, aren't they coy, these little writers of ours? But I knew he had a book in him and I knew that he knew. And that in the end he'd want it out – I mean, what's the point of working devotedly and modestly away in self-inflicted obscurity if nobody knows about it, eh? He wanted to be famously devoted, famously modest, famously obscure. (*caressing Jake*) And why shouldn't he? So, you see, if I could make a household name out of the likes of little Jake –

    Jake exits.

– you can imagine how easy my task was with those who were swollen with fame but ever greedy for more. Take any celebrity – even the great Rupert Rupertson – it wasn't enough that he was seen five times a week on television. He wanted us to see himself on the back of a book, too. A large photograph of . . .

Rupert has entered – Melon, continuing, speaks to him.

Rupert! Saw your programme the other night, by the way. Talking to the Russian ballerina. God, isn't she a stunner? Even Kate thought she was gorgeous. What happened afterwards?

Rupert After what?

Melon After the interview. Did you continue your investigation? Do report.

Rupert To the best of my knowledge, the BBC had her driven back to the Ritz, in a taxi.

Melon And you didn't go with her?

Rupert Look, Mark, I wish to Christ you'd understand. For some reason nature made me a one-woman man, and I've had mine. Since Gwen's death I've never wanted to make love to anybody else. I'm still in love with her, you see. Physically in love.

Melon Look, I *do* understand something of what you feel about Kate. I feel like that, up to a point, about Gwen. But –

Rupert The other way around, Mark.

Melon What?

Rupert Gwen was my wife. Kate's yours.

Melon Yes, a slip of the tongue, but on to what really matters. Had a chance to think it over yet? That little project I mentioned to you?

Rupert Yes. Yes, I have. But really I don't think an autobiography at my age. I'd never get away with it. After all, I'm only thirty-eight –

Melon Forty, isn't it? We're exactly the same age –

Rupert Yes, yes, yes, you're probably right, I don't keep close tally, you know, but whatever age I actually am, it's too young for an autobiography. Besides, they'd want details of my personal life, and since Gwen's death, I haven't had one. It's been work, work, work. But if I'm going to do a book, it's got to be the right one. Like some kind of tie-in on a documentary that I wouldn't just be fronting, but editing and writing.

Melon You know what we should do a book about? Death.

Rupert Death?

Melon Or more specifically – grief. Your grief. *The Public and Private Faces of Grief* – with lots of pictures of funerals, state funerals, family funerals, and running through it all, your face in close-up, your mouth, your eyes, full of the realisation of loss – the memories – I'd go with that, I really would. Think about it. Be in touch. Love to Kate, as always, eh! (*Turns to address the ladies.*) There your are, what did I tell you, easy as pie! The only problem with the Ruperts of the world is marketing them to their full potential. The only other problem is to trust them to, to –

> *Melon has been holding Rupert's face with his hand, squeezing hard. Rupert takes Melon's hand away and exits. Melon reads another card.*

'Tell them a little anecdote against yourself psychopath.' What? Who put –? Who put? Oh – A full stop after yourself. So it must mean tell them – that's you, ladies – a little anecdote against yourself. Then full stop. Then psychopath. So a little anecdote *about* a psychopath. But what psychopath? Which of my friends that I tried to get to write a book turned out to be a psycho –

Graeme has entered and sat in left chair – Melon continues.

Oh, of course! Graeme!

Graeme Mark!

Melon Long time no see.

Graeme Yes, I'm sorry I gave you such short notice, Mark. It's not easy to get away from Edinburgh at the moment, what with the various family problems, and the children, of course, but I decided I had to come and talk to you face to face. You remember when I first told you I was going to become a prison education officer, I felt I had a vocation for it, and you asked me to keep an eye out for a possible book?

Melon I think I said I'd be particularly interested in sex offenders. Particularly middle-class married ones.

Graeme Well, Angus Tait is not only a sex offender, but an all-round hard case. In fact, they don't come much harder. Which is why he's so remarkable. Angus Tait is almost certainly a psychopath, in my view. All his numerous acts of violence have been directed at obvious authority figures. Teachers, policemen, social workers needless to say, doctors, even clergymen.

Melon What did he do to them?

Graeme Well, for one thing he – I'd rather not go into the details, if you don't mind.

Melon Well, Graeme, details are of the essence. That would be the whole point of your book, wouldn't it?

Graeme Ah, there's a slight misunderstanding here. I'm not writing the book. He is. In fact, he's already done it. I've got it here with me, Mark. All three hundred pages, Mark.

Melon Good God – this could be even better – no offence, Graeme, but if it's any good – than a book for you!

Graeme Any good? Why do you think I'm here? It's a work of genius, Mark. Sheer genius! Here. Let me show you! Just take a glance – any page will give you the flavour – I couldn't write anything like this! Never!

Melon (*looks at the manuscript*) It – it seems to be a poem.

Graeme Exactly. But not just a poem, Mark. An epic poem.

Melon But it's in an odd sort of language. Not English –

Graeme No, it's a kind of patois. A mixture of Glaswegian – Gorbals – but mainly he's invented it. It only takes a line or two to get familiar with it, then you're away – there's a glossary at the back. Along with a map I drew up myself – so you can actually trace with your finger the whole saga of McBlone's journey.

Melon Here's the glossary, is it?

Graeme Why, what don't you understand?

Melon Well, only the title so far, actually.

Graeme No, no – as I said, just let yourself rip and it'll all make sense. Here – (*Takes the manuscript from Melon.*) Here. Any section – ah, yes, a great passage. A great, great passage. (*Begins to read.*)

> Ya wadna wee haach, on doon a bra
> Bae al yon totsle fra fern awa
> MacSleek and MacBlone.

MacSleek's the hero. MacBlone is the Lord of the Trumpets, half-god and half-darkness.

Melon Right.

Graeme (*reading*)
   MacSleek and MacBlone tagaether wee had
   An together thae made ta reight an the bad.
   Och the mad and tha bad,
   Tha bad and tha mad,
   But com awa bad
   An don head wit mad
   Fra MacSleek and MacBlone –

Melon (*holds up his hand to stop Graeme reading;*
Graeme stops.) His own stuff, of course. I realised that
the moment I looked at the manuscript. You see, he
hoped I'd agree to publish it because it was the work of
a psychopathic jailbird, and then he'd be able to say –

Graeme Well, I'm glad you like it, Mark, very glad. The
truth is, I wrote it myself, you see.

Melon No!

   Melon walks Graeme out as he continues.

Oh, if you knew these authors as I do, ladies, deceitful
in their deceptions, even, the stories I could tell you.
But what they all show is that I was a great publisher
who never, ever missed an opportunity, not a single
opportunity, however remote and improbable – not a
single *whiff* of an opportunity did I ever once miss –

   Josh has entered and sits on chair right. He is eating a
   yogurt.

Josh Hello, Dad.

Melon Ah, hello, Josh, where's Mum?

Josh She phoned. Said she had an examiners' meeting.
And can we make do with something from the fridge?

Melon Well, I can see you already have. Been in all evening?

Josh No, I went around to a friend for a bit.

Melon Ah. Which one?

Josh Oh, just someone from school. His name's Howard.

Melon And what did you do?

Josh Well, nothing really.

Melon I've often wondered how one does that. I've never managed it myself. It must require some special skill.

Josh Well, Howard – well, he wants to be a writer. And he's been keeping this diary, you see. Putting down day-to-day stuff about his mum and his new step-dad. He read it out to me, you see – and I thought that it should –

Melon (*interrupting*) Good. Did you manage to squeeze in a little work on your A levels before you went to Harold's?

Josh Well, a little. His name's Howard, Howard Skart, and I wondered if . . .

Melon (*interrupting*) Just because that school is expensive doesn't mean they'll get you into university unaided. You have to do a bit yourself, you know.

Josh I know, Dad. I did some. And I'll do some later. I really enjoyed it, Howard's diary. I thought some of it was really funny. In fact, I think it should be published.

Melon You know, that yogurt carton must be a miracle of packaging.

Josh looks at Melon questioningly.

You've already spooned down yourself three times as much as it looks as if it could contain.

Josh It's banana-flavoured.

Melon Ah, that explains it. Now, I'd better get on with some work. When are you going to do yours, exactly?

Josh After I get back from Howard's. He wants me to help pick out the best passages.

Melon You're not by any chance on drugs, are you, Josh?

Josh Drugs? No, why?

Melon Well, I'm beginning to think that such a complete lack of concern about your future can only be artificially induced.

Josh I'm not on drugs, Dad. I never have more than three or four joints a week. You know that. The thing about Howard's diary is . . .

Melon (*interrupting*) I believe you. I know you never lie to me. I mean, how can you? You don't use enough words to tell lies, eh? Just a joke, Josh.

Josh Oh. I told Howard you were a publisher, by the way. Hope you don't mind.

Melon You know, Josh – the brute fact is you won't get into university without two decent A levels. And then where will you be?

Josh Well, not in university, I suppose. (*Laughs, then continues.*) That was a joke, Dad. Sorry.

Melon A joke! A joke! (*Melon turns to audience.*) For a week or two I was the biggest bloody joke in London publishing. The dynamic, aggressive, never-miss-a-chance Mark Melon missing out on the best-seller of the year –

The Confessions of a Pubescent: the Diaries of Howard Skart, Age Sixteen – that – that his son, yes, his own son had actually tried to interest him in. But remember this, ladies, remember this, you ladies, you understand, don't you? You know what it's like trying to get through to your offspring. Especially when you're a man, and your offspring is a son! We're so busy trying to do our best by our hostages to fortune, so busy worrying about them, fretting for them, coaxing them, bullying, nagging them for their own good, for their *own* good, that when they do now and then break their silence what we listen for is the slur of drugs, the whine of the ambulance, the policeman's knock on the door. True? True? Of course it's true! But still I blame myself – there, sorry, at last I'm saying *sorry – sorry* that Harold – Howard, Howard Skart and his damned diaries had nine months at the top of the best-seller list! *Sorry* when the theatre version opened in the West End! *Sorry, sorry,* by God I was sorry when the television series went out, everywhere I looked – there was his face, Howard Skart's face, with his ridiculous glasses, those pubescent tufts on his upper lip and chin, and that smirk, above all that smirk – there it was in the newspaper advertisements, on posters in the Underground, on the sides of buses, everywhere I looked –

> *Josh wearing a T-shirt with the likeness of Howard Skart on it is eating as Melon speaks.*

What's that?

Josh Oh, gorp, dried fruit, nuts . . .

Melon No, no, not what you're eating, what you're wearing.

Josh Oh, it's a Skart T-shirt. Howard gave me a dozen.

Melon Well, that's lucky, isn't it, as you seem to have spilled gorp all over the face on that one.

Josh Oh, no. Those are meant to be his spots and blackheads.

Melon Ah. Oh, by the way, Josh – I've been meaning to ask. Why did you pass him on to Dominicus of all publishers?

Josh Well, because you used to work for them.

Melon And so?

Josh And so they're the only other publishers I'd ever heard of. Why? Aren't they any good?

Melon Well, they seem to be doing quite well at the moment. Thanks to Hector Skart and you.

Josh Yes, Howard says his agent says they've given him a really good deal on his next.

Melon Good, good. Well, um, I hope you're going to buckle down to it this evening, eh?

Josh Mmmm?

Melon To your A levels. After all, it's not your diary that's the top of the best-seller list, is it?

Josh Well, I'll just go and . . . just . . . (*Exits right.*)

Melon Oh, I know what you're thinking, ladies, you're thinking 'Oh, I do wish he'd stop punishing himself – and us – by going on and on about his one teeny-weeny mistake, good heavens, he's a famously successful publisher, let's have some upbeat, some lift-off, let's hear about his almost legendary feats of alchemy, how he took hold of a lump of pure gold and transformed it in a jiffy into a lump of base metal' –

Josh appears in window right.

That's what you're – No, no, a lump of base metal and transformed it into pure gold. *That's* alchemy. The other way around is what we do most of the time. With our lives, eh? Josh . . . Josh!

Makes to go to Josh, who disappears. Melon stops, stares out, looks down at cards.

On to the next. On to the next. 'Modes of distribution. Transport cost efficiency. Illustrate comparative percentages, Swanage, Huddersfield. Keep lively.' Now, ladies, if you consider the location of our two warehouses when I arrived at Haylife and Gladstone, the one in Swanage and the one in Huddersfield, and then consider them in their relationship to our major market, which was, of course, London, soon to include New York, Boston, Sydney, Melbourne, Toronto, Montreal, and so forth, so forth, so forth – you'll understand – understand why I – I – I insisted. To. The. Powers. That. Be. Powers. That. Be. In accounts, that is –

Gladys has entered and stands at Melon's left. He turns to her and offers his hand.

Miss Powers! Thank you so much for coming to see me.

Gladys No, no, thank you for – for – actually the name is Wiggins. Mrs Wiggins. But I thought Powers would make a – a –

Melon Good *nom de plume*. Or *nom de guerre* even. And so it does. Well, please sit down, Mrs – no, I'll stick with Powers and Miss. So please sit down, Miss Powers.

Gladys Thank you.

She sits on chair left, Melon chair right.

Melon Look, let's pass on the preliminary courtesies, shall we, Miss Powers? Let's get straight to the point. As we both know what it is I've asked you here to talk about. *The Madonna in Chains*. Interesting title.

Gladys I've made up a list of six or seven others – *Phyllis Unleashed* is one, and *Uncuff Me, Sir!* – that's with an exclamation mark and *Gladys in* – I mean *Phyllis in Bondage,* and several more, most of them with her name in, perhaps it's better just to call it *Phyllis*, straight out.

Melon *Phyllis Straight Out?*

Gladys No, come straight out with it and call it *Phyllis*, as she's what my novel's about, after all.

Melon Look, Miss Powers – can I call you Gladys?

Gladys Yes. Yes, please do. Yes.

Melon I'm Mark.

Gladys Mark. Yes.

Melon Listen, Gladys, we won't get anywhere unless we're absolutely honest with each other.

Gladys I agree. Go on, Mark.

Melon Who else has seen it?

Gladys Well, almost every publisher I could find out about.

Melon What did they say?

Gladys The ones who bothered to say anything said it's terrible. The dialogue's feeble, there isn't a proper plot, and I have an eye for the sort of detail that doesn't count.

Melon And what do you think?

Gladys I think I have an important talent.

Melon So do I, Gladys.

Gladys Go on, Mark, please.

Melon We've had an amazing stroke of luck, Gladys, you and I. I just happened to see it on my fiction editor's desk when he wasn't there. I glanced into it and then made off with it because I'd opened it at the right page, as it turned out. I couldn't stop reading. I was aroused – frankly aroused. Had an erection. Never came across anything like it. Simultaneously erotic and ill-natured. Self-righteous pornography, that's what it is.

Gladys Thank you, Mark.

Melon Of course, when I went back and read the beginning, and then forward to read the end, I realised he was right, our fiction editor, as were all the other publishers. It's hopeless as a novel. Quite hopeless. A penis-shriveller.

Gladys Go on, Mark.

Melon If we stuck to the middle section, from where you write as yourself about what a woman experiences when she lusts for a man, what happens to you physically, what happens in your imagination – your sense of humiliation, Phyllis –

Gladys Gladys, don't you mean, Mark?

Melon Yes, of course. Gladys, I mean, Phyllis. I mean Gladys, I mean Gladys.

Gladys I wrote that whole bit when I'd had too much sherry. The rest of it I thought about.

Melon Then give up thinking and stick to the sherry.

Gladys I will. Yes, I will, Mark.

Melon I'll do it in hardback and paperback simultaneously and I'll get them on the market six months sooner than is humanly possible. We'll keep agents out of it, and speak to each other direct. When you know more about these things, you'll understand that that's a very good deal. But you don't have to give me your decision right away. Take your time to think about it, Phyllis.

Gladys Very well, Mark, I will. It's Gladys.

Melon Gladys. And what does your husband, Mr Wiggins, think of your book?

Gladys He says it all stinks except for the middle bit. It gave him an erection, too.

Melon What does he do?

Gladys He's a policeman.

Melon I'll bet he's a damn good one.

Gladys Well, he's very good at arresting people but very bad at giving evidence against them. He doesn't know how to make things up, you see. However hard he tries, the juries always know he's lying, poor dear. He's my ex-husband, by the way.

Melon Is he, indeed? We'll have lunch, then, shall we? One day next week? You can give me your decision.

Gladys I'd like that, Mark. Thank you. But you probably already know my decision.

Melon The lunch will be to celebrate it. Next week, then.

Gladys Next week, Mark. (*Exits.*)

Melon So what did I do, what did I do to relieve myself of the throbbing, almost sobbing – my lust for Gladys – my excitement at the deal I knew I was going to pull off –

because I knew, yes knew in my publisher's bones, my publisher's loins – what did I do? Oh, of *course! (Begins to undress.)* What every man does – given that any man could look at a lump of dross called *Madonna in Chains* and convert it into a best-selling nugget of pure gold called *Gladys Unbound* – the usual thing – the quite routine thing whatever state I was in. Sammy, love, come in and take a memo.

Samantha enters.

Ah, poppet, there you are at last. What kept you?

Samantha In one of your excitements, are you?

Melon Yes, yes, take a memo, poppet. Take lots of memos. No, don't take any memos. We're about to have a celebration. I'm giving you a forty-five-minute tea break.

Samantha Tea break from what? I finish work in five minutes.

Melon Then I'm giving you a five-minute tea break.

Samantha Five minutes!

Melon And forty minutes of overtime. An hour if you want. I'm in the mood for whatever you like this evening, poppet.

Samantha What I'd like is for you to go through my essay on *Twelfth Night* with me.

Melon Then I shall. We'll fit in an extra twenty minutes when we're done. (*He begins to undress her.*)

Samantha But you've got to be at the Savoy in an hour exactly.

Melon The Savoy? Why do I have to be at the Savoy?

Samantha To meet Mr McKinley, the Canadian sales representative.

Melon Oh yes. Of course. To fire him. This is for reminding me – (*He kisses her.*) God, what a treasure you are, Sammy poppet. (*Continues undressing her.*)

Samantha But I've got to hand *Twelfth Night* in this evening. And I only got a B-minus for the *Macbeth* we did last week.

Melon Probably my fault. Never could work out those bloody witches. But what's the point of my getting you into university, Sammy, what will happen to me, tell me that?

Samantha Oh, you'll always find someone for your office pokes. That new tea-girl wouldn't mind a go, for instance.

Melon Really? How do you know?

Samantha Because the other day I heard her saying she fancied somebody absolutely rotten. And who could that be but you? (*He has removed almost all of her clothing.*) Aren't you going to take the rest off? I hate standing around looking like something from a dirty magazine.

Melon First we kiss poppet's lovely shoulder – (*Does so.*) Then we kiss poppet's pretty breasts – (*Does so.*) And then poppet's delicious navel – (*Does so.*) And then poppet's delicious memo pad – (*Does so.*) Ah, poppet, ah, love.

They lower to the floor.

Samantha Oh, my Mark!

Melon Oh poppet, oh, love, oh, poppet!

Samantha Oh, Mark, Mark, my Mark!

During this love-making, Kate has entered and sat in chair right. Melon looks up, sees her, gets to his feet as he speaks.

Melon Hello, Kate, love. I like that dress, when did you get it?

Samantha lies still for a moment, then slowly sits up, beginning to gather her things.

Kate Oh – about two years ago, I think. I decided to keep on wearing it until you noticed it.

Melon Then your patience has paid off. God, what a day!

Kate Oh, bad then, was it?

Melon No, great! A great day, Kate, love. A bit of the usual arsing about with old-bore-and-old-nuisance and young beaten-down-by-life and then on to Gladys Powers.

Kate What happened? Did you sign her up?

Melon Sign her up? I hog-tied her. Then I . . .

Momentarily, Melon and Samantha look at each other. He continues speaking as she continues to gather her things, then exits.

. . . went on to the Savoy. Dinner with McKinley. The Canadian rep. Sacked him. And what about you, what sort of day did you have, my love? What sort of day?

Kate You really must calm down, darling. *Calm down.* You look as if you're going to explode.

Melon You're right, love, you're right. Adrenalin's been flowing ever since I lassoed Gladys, slung her over my horse, and galloped her off to the best-seller list.

Kate Now sit down. Sit down. Ask me again.

Melon (*sits on Kate's knee*) Ask you what?

Kate What sort of day I've had.

Melon Tell me, love, what sort of day have you had?

Kate You won't want to hear about it. Too dull.

Melon Thank you.

Kate Oh! Except for the examiners' meeting. That got nasty. So I thought of you.

Melon Of me. Thank you, love. Why?

Kate The question was whether we should set up a course on misogyny and the English male.

Melon And what did you decide?

Kate Well, as I say, I thought of you. And explained to my English colleagues that as their males were already misogynists, they didn't need a course.

Melon (*begins to undo buttons on Kate's dress*) Tell me, my love, did you put this on for him too?

Kate Mmmm?

Melon For your lover, love. Which of us did you wear it for?

Kate Oh, not for you as you've never noticed it. And not for him, because he noticed it the first time I wore it, so I could never wear it again, could I, for him?

Melon So what do you wear for him?

Kate What I wear for you. Until he notices. Which is almost at once.

Melon So you have to wear a new outfit every time you see him?

Kate That's right. That's why you and I have to work so hard. To keep me in new clothes.

Melon So he likes you to look sexy for him, does he?

Kate Of course he does. Don't you?

Melon What, like you to look sexy for him?

Kate No. For you.

Melon But how can I tell that when you're looking sexy you're looking sexy for me? Perhaps you're thinking about him.

Kate Or it could be the other way around. When I'm with him, looking sexy, I'm thinking about you. Come on, you can finish me off in the bedroom, I've got an examiners' meeting at nine tomorrow –

Melon Do you love him more?

Kate More?

Melon More than you love me.

Kate I could never love any man more than I love you. He doesn't exist, my lover, darling, thank God. He's just a game we play. Now don't forget. So come to bed.

Melon Just one more question.

Kate Only one, then.

Melon Does he dare do all that becomes a man?

Kate Who dares do more is none. So come to bed, my man, and be a husband.

> *They exit up centre. Recorded voice of Melon: 'Oh, my love – my darling, Kate.' Followed by recorded voice of Kate: 'Oh, oh my sweet – my darling, darling darling' – followed by recorded sounds of love-making followed by snores. Melon speaks to the silence.*

So he's real then, is he, love? Your lover, eh, love? I know
he is – I know he is, love – because he's here now all
right – making love to you. I can see him, I can hear
him, I can smell him – in here – (*tapping his head*) – in
here . . .

> *The alarm clock goes off – Melon finds it, turns it off
> and speaks to the ladies.*

I warned them I wasn't ready, said I'd get caught up and
certain things would tumble out – but no, they said, no
those bloody doctors said go on, just a pack of old ladies
in Cheltenham, Chelmsford, Chippendale, Chislehurst,
wherever, so look them straight in the eye and stick to
your cards, but there you are, aren't you, making your
judgements, despising me. Well, well, go ahead, go
ahead, judge and despise, but remember – I'm telling
you – no, you tell me, you – you ladies out there, what
harm did I do, what harm did we do, however often
I did it, with however many – just because I had a
perfectly easy, relaxed, healthy liking – yes, that's the
word, *healthy* liking. And relaxed. And good. And so
forth. And so forth. And so forth. What harm? I didn't.
None. No harm at all. I merely let the emotions rip *and*
brought into play all kinds of muscles you don't use on
the tennis courts, even some – certainly one – you don't
use in swimming. Hey, where are you going? You, the
plump lady there waddling towards the exit, hey there,
fattie, where are you off to, back home to your dreary,
faithless hubby? Do you think he's any different, do you
think he hasn't had his poppet, his poppet? And you –
you spindle-shanks, oh, and look, flounce, flounce,
flounce, look at them – the one with the carrier bag! See
her – do you know what they can't bear? That my Kate
and I were happy! That's what they can't bear. That on
top of everything else I had a happy marriage. No – no –
you there, how dare you push your way through like

that. You bloody sit down, sit down, you old cow, do you hear me! Sit down and get it into your skulls that whatever you might think, I was that rare thing, a happy man. A happy, happy, happy man. Oh God, I was happy! (*Stares at the ladies then looks down and sees that he is not clothed.*) But where are my trousers, why am I undressed, where are my clothes? Oh God, I'm sorry, I'm so sorry. Please forgive me, ladies, please, please forgive me. (*Begins to sob.*)

Act Two

Melon Thank you, thank you, the lady in the blue hat –
such a charming hat – for the Kleenex. But first I
mustn't forget this – (*Takes out and re-sets alarm clock.*)
It did splendid service the first round, didn't it, beloved
old thing – present, you know, a present from a beloved
– so we can trust it to bring me to heel in the second
round. I mustn't overstep the mark, must I, ladies, and
keep you from all your duties. You have husbands to get
home to, meals to prepare – oh, and there's this – (*Takes
a piece of paper from his pocket.*) which Mrs Macdonald
asked me to read out. News – and very exciting news,
it seems too – about next week's talk. Perhaps I should
keep that for the end so that we can close on a note of
anticipation. Now. Perhaps you'd like to move forward
and fill all those now empty chairs at the front. I shan't
be shouting at you any more, shall I, as you've asked me
not to and – and – to be quite frank my voice – I think
I'm having trouble making myself heard. (*Blows his nose
and surveys them.*) There. That's better, isn't it? Now
I feel I'm just sitting among friends. In a cosy little
group. And I can talk at last intimately and naturally
and – as you'd like me to talk to you. As you told me
you would. No boasting. No shouting. No lying. No, no.
Just the truth. But you see, ladies, please believe me, you
must believe me, please when I say: that I still don't
know what the truth is. No, I don't. That's still my
problem. That I've had the experience, you see. But
as the poet, some poet, famous poet said, had the
experience but missed the meaning. No. He'd had the
meaning but missed the experience. So it was – in my

264

case it was – exactly the opposite of what some famous
poet said. If he was famous. Was a poet even. Not that it
matters. What matters for me, even now, is that for me,
experience has no meaning. Now I know – yes, I know,
from what one or two of you were kind enough to
whisper to me at tea-time, Miss – Miss – and the lady
there, and you, too, madam, that you'd become rather
intrigued by – by the nature of my marriage. Wanted to
hear more about it. What went on behind the bedroom
door, eh? No, no, please don't be embarrassed, after all
there's no doubt that in the end my – my – what word
would you like me to use, ladies? Bonking? May I try
bonking to see if I can catch the – the proper note for
what I did? Thank you. Well, there's no doubt that my
tendency to bonk whomever whenever wherever I could
played – no, became somehow involved in what
eventually befell me, and it would be satisfying, wouldn't
it, you'd be satisfied, a lot of people would be satisfied,
why even I – yes I would, ladies – would be satisfied if I
felt that my – fate, I suppose it was, was the consequence
of a bonk-bonk here, a bonk-bonk there, here a bonk,
there a bonk, everywhere a bonk-bonk. Again – sorry.
And sorry for the sorry. Perhaps the word bonk leads
one into a certain onomatopoeic – which means, I
should just explain, a word that sounds like or enacts the
action it describes, if I recall correctly, as with say . . .
say, yes whipping, *whip* . . . whip! Whipping – you hear
it, hear the noise through the air, don't you, ladies, eh?
Well, with bonking – bonking –

> *Kate enters from up centre and very slowly makes her
> way to the chair right to sit. She does up the front of
> her dress.*

– no, it's not really the same, is it? Not onomatopoeic
at all. I mean bonk isn't like – like – doesn't enact the
action. I must say, I do rather miss those little cards, that

I discarded, even though there almost certainly wouldn't have been one that would have helped me get away from bonking and on to – on to what I was trying to explain about my – my . . . (*to Kate*) But what's the matter with you, love? Is there something you've been up to, have you been up to something again with your lover, love? But you look so sad, love, and frightened. What's been going on? Have you and he done something that's frightened you? Tell me, you can tell me, I won't mind knowing. Nothing you could do could ever – no, love, not ever – even with him. So tell me . . . tell me . . . tell me . . .

Michael enters carrying an envelope.

Michael Mark, a word if you please about this package – this package of pornography you sent to me. To my home. For *Further Masturbation without Shame*.
I thought you'd like to know – like to know – that Melissa opened it – and as poor little Marcus was in one of his tantrums he knocked it out of her hand – and there they were – scattered all over the floor, picture after picture of homosexual men and women doing vile – unspeakable – unspeakable things to each other! And then poor little Marcus actually – actually picked them up, grabbed them up before we could stop him and – and –

Melon Oh, don't tell me, Michael! Got his sticky little fingers all over them! But don't worry – don't worry – I shan't say a word to Edward about it.

Michael Edward?

Melon Well, they were from him, you see, and as he went to a lot of trouble finding them, he'd be a bit upset if he found out they'd been messed up even though it was obviously an accident.

Michael And did Edward explain what *use* he thought I'd make of this filth? Did he?

Melon Well, I *think* he's got it into his head that you're not being serious enough about *Further Masturbation without Shame*.

Michael Shame, shame, yes, that's the word, shame – has he lost all sense of it, all sense of shame that this house – this house – his house – the great names that he boasts of – Yeats, Eliot, Ezra Pound should – should roll about in the gutter – in the gutter? I don't think I have anything to offer to *this* house any longer.

Melon Now calm down, Michael – let's not be hasty, let's not be rash. Let's think this through logically. You're asking what you have to offer this house? Haylife and Gladstone needs a man who can take conventional wisdom and turn it on its head, a creator of the unorthodox, the bold, the daring – a genius, in other words. And thank God we have that – the necessary genius – in me.

Michael I thought we were talking about what I have to offer.

Melon I'm coming to that. What you have to offer is a very rare quality indeed, Michael. Blind obedience to your true master.

Michael Master!? My true master?

Melon That's what I pay you such generous – overgenerous I sometimes think – wages for. But I realise you need them, if you're going to send little Marcus to the kind of school that'll keep him out of your way and leave you with a clear conscience, rather than having him forcibly removed to a state-run correctional institution – and then perhaps you could get rid of Melissa, too.

Michael What? What are you saying?

Melon I've got great plans, Michael – and you're included in them. We're going to diversify. We're going into ice-skating shows. Restaurants. Chinese, Indian, Greek. Dry-cleaning. At the moment I'm keeping a close eye on brickles.

Michael Brickles, brickles, brickles – and what the hell – what the bloody hell are brickles? True master?

Melon Up three per cent on last week. Otherwise don't worry your faithful little head about what brickles are.

Michael You're mad! You've gone completely mad. I have no choice but to offer my resignation.

Gladstone (*enters, sees Michael*) Oh, I'll come back when you're free, Mark.

Michael (*to Gladstone as he hands him the envelope*) Just a moment, Edward. These belong to you, I believe. You filthy old man.

Gladstone (*taking envelope*) Oh, thank you very much, young man. I'm frightfully busy right now. I'll read them later. (*Exits.*)

Michael (*to Melon*) My resignation will be on your desk in ten minutes.

Melon Oh Michael, no, please make it five . . .

Michael exits.

(*calling*) Poppet . . . poppet . . . come and take a memo!

Gladys enters and sits on chair left.

Gladys I've just dropped in to tell you, Mark, that I've got myself an agent after all. He tells me that you actually swindled me on our original contract. He's

268

sending my new book, *Phyllis* . . . I mean *Gladys, Part Two: The Chastity Belt,* to another publisher.

Melon Congratulations. So you've come of age at last . . . Gladys, thank God. Now I can collect.

Gladys Collect? What is there left for you to collect?

Melon What I collect from all my lady authors in the end. A fuck, Gladys, because I've earned it. You see, I'm your alchemist. Yes, your alchemist. I took your dross and turned it into gold. And all I ask in return is a fuck whenever I need it. Look, we'll have lunch followed by a session at the Charing Cross Hotel. We'll dance together naked in our little bedroom before you slip into something indecent and we begin our games. Oh, what games we'll have, Gladys! I'll spank your bare bottom and tie you to the bedpost – your wrists – your ankles –

Gladys Thank you very much, Mark, but you see, I've never had the slightest interest in sex except as a literary topic. (*Exits.*)

Melon That's why I want to fuck you, fuck you, fuck you . . . Sammy, poppet, I need my memo.

Samantha enters.

There you are. What kept you? (*Lowers his trousers.*)

Samantha What are you doing?

Melon What do you mean, what am I doing? You know perfectly well what I'm doing. What I always do.

Samantha But you've just done it.

Melon You mean – you mean we've already –?

Samantha You really don't remember? But how could you – even you? Either you're lying, Mark, or there's something wrong with you and you ought to see someone. A doctor even.

Melon Oh come on, Sammy, you mustn't be upset. We do it so often that I probably didn't even notice. Like having a cup of coffee, eh, love? And now I fancy another one.

Samantha Don't you touch me, don't you dare touch me! I don't want it ever again – sex like a cup of coffee, Mark – sex that you don't remember. With your poppet – your poppet.

Samantha exits as Melon follows, trousers round his ankles.

Melon Oh come on, Sammy – just a quick dip. One for the road to see me home. (*Pulls up his trousers while speaking.*) Oh, women, women, bloody women! You're all the same.

Jacob enters.

A bit of fun in the afternoon and you turn it into some sort of sacred ritual, eh, ladies? (*Turns to see Jacob.*) Oh hello, Jake. How's your sex life? Young Donald still giving you decent service?

Jacob Who's Donald?

Melon Who is it then, works in a Turkish bath, moved into your place a few weeks ago?

Jacob David. He works at the box office at the National Theatre. Interesting.

Melon What?

Jacob Your contempt for homosexuals, Mark.

Melon Contempt! What do you mean, contempt? Even if you do put the part of the body I most admire into the part for which I have the least respect! No, no, your problem isn't that you're a queer but that you're a Jew. However much you may want the sex, all you let yourself think about is love. And when it's not love, it's shame and retribution. Face it, Jake, your cock is still under orders from the Old Testament.

Jacob You're evidently on the way to becoming very sick, Mark. And that's a professional opinion. I can't treat you myself, of course, but I can give you the names of some very good people . . .

Melon Fuck off, Jake.

Jacob Very well, Mark, if that's what you want.

Melon Yes it is what I want – so fuck off fuck off fuck off fuck off . . .

Jacob exits left.

Professional opinion – professional opinion – I made him a household name but all he's really good for is aspirin-peddling and looney-coddling down in the East End, dishing out nosedrops to people with colds while they whine on about their jobs, their lack of jobs, their illegitimate babies, their legitimate babies, their wife-battering husbands, their incompetent sex-denying wives. He's never known what it's like to encounter a sane, robustly healthy, cheerful, fun-loving prankster of an Englishman, isn't that right, ladies?

Graeme has entered right.

Oh . . . hello, Graeme, what do you want?

Graeme What do I want? But you asked me here.

Melon What?

Graeme But don't you remember? You phoned me in
Edinburgh last night. After midnight. Woke the whole
household up. You said it was absolutely urgent, Mark!
A matter of life and death.

Melon Good God, yes of course. And I was right. It is!

Graeme Well, here I am . . . at your disposal, Mark.

Melon I've written something especially for you. In fact,
I'm going to dedicate it to you, my favourite epic poet.
It's called 'The Ballad of McTit and McTwat.' (*in
Scottish accent*)

> Oh here is a tale of McTit and McTwat,
> T'wan small and firrum,
> T'other long an' fat.
> Nah McTit and McTwat tagathurr they
> Ta whoole of a wahman
> Reet doon to ta pee.

Melon chases Graeme off the stage.

Oh, I can see what you're thinking, ladies, you're
thinking, 'What a very silly, very naughty boy!' What he
needs is a good slap on the bottom, then off to bed with
him, eh? No, no of course you're not. You're not
thinking that at all, are you? You're thinking that I must
have gone bonkers, aren't you? Bonkers. Did we decide –
did we decide that I mustn't use that word any more?
No, no, it was the verb we turned against, wasn't it?
No more bonking. But bonkers acceptable. As a word,
that is. Not as a condition, of course. Bonking, the verb,
out. Bonkers, the adjective, in. Odd though, isn't it,
I can't think of any other adjectives that end in *ers*. Can
you? *Ers – ers –* bonkers – Crackers. There's another
one. Bonkers and crackers. Now isn't that a coincidence?
Because that's exactly what I was, wasn't I, two adjectives
ending in *ers*, absolutely bonkers. Completely crackers.

And how much further could I go then to be absolutely
and completely *ers*, bonk and crack, eh, ladies. And so
forth. So forth and so forth and so forth and so forth
and – and . . . Now where were we? You know, if things
had been different I'd be pulling out one of those little
cards about now again, wouldn't I? Preferably the one
about Swanage and London, Huddersfield and London,
ratio of distance to cost-efficiency factors, and how I –
I – I single-handedly managed to merge our Huddersfield
and Swanage depots into one depot at Watford,
branching in south to London, branching out north to –
to Huddersfield. Can that be right? But what would have
been the point of that? That wouldn't have been cost-
effective, that would have been – would have been –
both economically unfeasible and unviable economically,
so what exactly did I do that transformed the whole
transport structure – that saved us three quarters of a
million, put us in the black? What did I do, love – (*to
Kate*) – that turned the whole thing around, transformed
us in the course of an evening from a playful, cheerful,
happy, happy – yes, above all we were happy, weren't
we, love? – until he suddenly popped up between us.
And turned everything around. And ruined everything.
What did I do? Where did he come from? Your lover,
love. He was just a game, a fiction, a pretence, a little
itch we created for ourselves to scratch when we
wanted. Foreplay – our little bit of foreplay. For years
and years. So why suddenly did he – without
explanation – how did he – get into our lives? Out of
our game and into my brain. And out of my brain into
our lives? What was his trick? How did he manage it,
your lover? That's what we all need to know. So tell me,
tell me, tell me. I need to know. Tell me. Tell me, love,
tell me, Kate love, who he is and why you let him, love!
That's all I need to know, love, eh love?

Josh has entered left and sat in left chair, noisily eating cornflakes. Melon turns to Josh and speaks to him.

What's that you're eating?

Josh Cornflakes.

Melon I thought cornflakes were for breakfast.

Josh mumbles something inaudible.

What? What did you say?

Josh I said, well, yes.

Melon To what?

Josh To cornflakes being for breakfast.

Melon But it's nearly seven o'clock. In the evening. What we have outside this house is twilight. Not dawn. They're different things. Almost opposites, in some respects. So why are you eating cornflakes at twilight when, according to your own statement, you take them for breakfast, which everybody knows follows on after the dawn? Eh? Eh?

Josh I only just got up.

Melon Why?

Josh Didn't get to sleep all night.

Melon Why? I'm waiting.

Josh Lot of noise.

Melon Indeed? What sort of noise?

Josh From your bedroom. You and Mum talking, I suppose.

Melon Suppose? What do you mean suppose? Who else would you expect to hear in our bedroom all night but me and Mum. Eh?

Josh Well, nobody.

Melon Have you ever heard anybody but me talking with Mum in our bedroom?

Josh Well – only the cleaning woman.

Melon The cleaning woman? Has it ever crossed your mind that she might be – lesbian?

Josh Who?

Melon The cleaning woman.

Josh Lesbian?

Melon Why not? Stranger things.

Josh Well, she's a granny, isn't she?

Melon Nonsense. She's young and black, pretty and enlightened. One knows the type. Active. Radical. Gay rights. Possibly a dyke. Why not?

Josh That was the one before last. The student. Filling in.

Melon Where are you going?

Josh Nowhere. To get an apple.

Melon Oh, you think that's where they come from, do you, just like the food in the fridge, the clothes on your back, the money in your pocket, a modern youth's version of it all growing on trees, eh – nowhere? Appropriate, as it's even stupider and vaguely nasty and justifies taking as much as you want whenever you want it. Well, grasp this, grasp this, it comes from *me*. *I* provide it, I work to provide it. I'm a great worker, that's why I'm a great provider, I provide evening cornflakes for my son, and apples at dawn for my son, and friends for my wife and my wife for my friends, so sit down – sit down! And you bloody well answer my question.

Josh What question?

Melon Who is it? Who is it? Who is it, who is it, who is it . . .?

Melon grabs at Josh, who tries to escape as Melon chases after him. Josh exits left. At up-left centre, Melon speaks.

It's one of my friends, isn't it, love?

Kate Now listen, darling, listen. It isn't one of your friends, it isn't anyone. I've never had a lover. He's a fiction. You made him up. You.

Melon But why would I do that, love?

Kate I don't know, my darling. For fun. It was – it was part of your foreplay. For ages. It's in your head that he existed. Nowhere else.

Melon Then how has he got out of it and into our lives? How did he manage it, love, if he didn't really exist? Because he's there now all right. Here now all right. I can see him, I can hear him, I can smell him making love to you.

Kate You're very ill, my darling. Everybody knows it – Jacob, Graeme, Michael, Rupert – even Gladys. They all know you're ill. And that's how he got out of your head. Because of your illness. That's who he is – my lover. He's your illness.

Melon That's not true, Kate. We both know that isn't true. Are you afraid I'll be angry again? I won't be angry any more, I promise. Just tell me which of my friends it is, that's all. That's all, Kate.

Kate Oh God, oh God.

Melon What?

Kate I've got a job to do, work to do, a life to get on with. Can't you see – can't you see what's happened to you?

Melon Yes – yes, something, something. But if you just tell me I'd be all right. Tell me. Tell me which of my friends it is. It's him, isn't it?

Kate Oh, him. Yes. A very likely candidate. A perfectly reasonable choice. Him. Congratulations.

Melon So it's him.

Kate And if I said no?

Melon You'd by lying, Kate, my love. Now I know it's him, I *know* it's him. He is your bloke as – as I'm your husband. As surely as that.

Kate And there's nothing surer than that, Mark. Is there?

Melon Just say it then. Then we'll be finished. It's all I've ever wanted. Just to know. That's all.

Kate But you say you do know.

Melon I still need you to say it, love. Then we can all rest. Just say it's him, just say it, please.

Kate Very well, I'll say it. It's him.

Melon Oh, thank you. Thank you, love. Already I feel much better. So much better.

Kate Good. Then I'll just go and – and rest at last. Such a hard day tomorrow. Such a hard day.

Melon One thing, love. Just one thing. How often did you do it, you and he?

Kate We agreed that once I said it – you said that once I'd said it was him, we'd rest.

Melon But we are resting, love. Look at us. I just want to know whether you love him, that's all. No harm in that, surely?

Kate I have never loved anybody but you. Is there any point in my saying that I have never slept with anybody but you?

Melon It's too late, Kate. You can't go back now. You've already confessed.

Kate I've confessed nothing. Nothing. There's nothing to confess! You're mad, don't you see, you're mad! You need help. You must get help.

Melon I'm not mad, love. Not any longer. I just want to get to the bottom of this. Why did you and he become lovers? Was it because of my little adventures? Because I had them you wanted them too?

Kate Your little adventures? What do you mean?

Melon My little flings. With secretaries and Gladys and ladies here and there in publishing.

Kate Your little flings? Secretaries and Gladys – Gladys! You mean you've been unfaithful to me? All this! And *you've* been unfaithful to me? And with Gladys!

Melon Actually not Gladys, come to think of it. She turned me down. But it doesn't matter because they didn't mean anything to me. Not any of them. Not even my poppet. That's the difference. While you and he for ages, you said – you said yourself, for ages –

that's something else entirely. That's a kind of love,
you see. Yours and his. His and yours.

Kate Little flings, little adventures, your poppet and
Gladys, who turned you down.

Melon It's not funny, love! Oh, it's not funny!
You've got to tell me. You've got to tell me.

Kate Tell you what? What is there left to tell? Now we
both know everything.

Melon Did you love him more? That's what I need to
know. Did you love him more? What sort of things did
you do together. In his bed? In our bed? Did you go to
restaurants? Hotels? In the afternoon? How many people
saw you? How many people know? Who have you told?
Who has he told? Does everybody know? Am I the only
one – am I the last – the last – am I? Am I? Just answer
that one question. That's all I ask. Do you love him more?
More? Oh God, oh God – Kate . . . Kate . . . Kate . . .
Do you love him more . . .? Do you love him more . . .?

Gladstone (*entering*) Mark, Mark, I just remembered –
I keep forgetting to tell you that wonderful story about
Ezra Pound. He spent a week staying with the Duke of
Sussex, you see, and when he left, getting into the train,
he leaned out of the window and said to the Duke, 'You
know, it's been a wonderful week – good food, the
relaxed company, the country air. And – furthermore
I just want you to know that your wife is the greatest
fuck in England.' And the train pulled out and an
elderly gentleman said, 'Did you really just say, sir – did
you really just say that about his wife?' and Ezra said,
'I know, I know, she's a dreadful fuck, but he's such a
sweet, kind old chap that I wanted to be sweet and kind
back.' (*Laughs.*)

279

Melon Do you really think it's funny? A man betraying his host, taking his wife – you think that's funny. Oh, you old – you old . . .

Melon chases Gladstone out, off left. Rupert enters from right to Kate, then crosses upstage to meet Melon at left. They walk downstage to just right of centre.

You've seen her today, haven't you, Rupert?

Rupert Yes. I have.

Melon You know how I know. I saw you in here. (*tapping his head.*) Whispering and kissing.

Rupert We were talking about you. She asked me to meet her to talk about you.

Melon Did she?

Rupert Yes. She wants me to assure you that we're not having and have never had an affair. Well, that's really it.

Melon Really what?

Rupert Kate and I have never had an affair. That's it. The whole story. There isn't one, Mark. Alas!

Melon Alas? What do you mean 'Alas', Rupert?

Rupert Nothing – only that I've always admired Kate enormously. But as you know better than anyone, I'm a one-woman man and I've had mine. But this is no place for Gwen. Look, Mark, we all of us, all your friends, Kate, all of us, Jacob especially, who knows about these things – we all know that what's happened to you is not your fault, Mark, but you've really got to get help. For Kate's sake as much as for your own –

Melon God, how you must have loved it, weeping about your dead wife while all the time you were fucking mine!

(*He grabs Rupert's face hard.*) Oh you sod, you sod, you treacherous, pious, hypocritical . . .

> *Melon releases his grip and falls to the floor, on all fours as Rupert exits. Melon turns to the audience.*

Really, ladies, I do promise you, there's not much more of this to go. A few more skirmishes, a tussle here and there. Restaurants were bad places for me at this period, by the way. I always seemed to end the evening just after the main course, rolling about the floor, yelping, thus giving the impression that the fault was in the kitchens. Very unfair on the chefs – I was banned, actually, from quite a few – but what impresses me now – I can say it, ladies, without fear or favour – now that I've been so honest and direct and truthful and so forth and so forth and so forth, just as I promised after tea, and so forth was – was – (*to Kate*) – you must help me. Please.

Kate Get up. You mustn't be down there on your hands and knees like a dog. It's not . . . becoming, Mark.

Melon Love me, please. That's all I ask. Love me.

Kate I will, I will, oh I will! If only you'll help me.

Melon Oh yes, yes. Anything. Just tell me what it is. I'll do anything to help you.

Kate Then see someone who can help you. And then you'll be helping me, you see.

Melon Who? Who is this someone?

Kate If you do, then I'll be able to love you again. I know I will.

Melon I love you, I love you.

Kate Then come with me.

Melon I can't. I want to be with you. I have to be with you.

Kate I'm always with you, darling. You know that. (*Gets Melon to his feet.*) Come, my darling, come. And everything will be all right, you'll see.

> *She has walked Melon upstage. As they get to centre opening she snatches her hand away and disappears off right.*

Melon Kate! Kate! Kate!

> *Melon falls to the floor and begins to crawl downstage as Shrink 1 enters from left to sit in left chair as Shrink 2 enters from right and sits right.*

Shrink 1 And then I said, what do you think this is? A lay-by for layabouts? Last week you didn't exist for me. Last week you were failing somewhere else with some other psychiatrist. You're a bit of a gadabout when it comes to failure, Mr Melon. You like to fail all over the place. And of course, he said, but I said, health isn't a gift. It has to be earned. You must work to be cured, Mr Melon. I can't remember how long it took to hose down the Augean stables but, by general consent, your psyche is in a fouler state than they were. We'll do our best. Even if you're not good enough. That's all for today. Time's up. Bill's in the post. Let's hope that tomorrow the cheque will be, eh?

Shrink 2 And I said, tell me, Mr Melon, how many do you smoke? So of course he said, so I said, but you've smoked ten while we've been talking. You've smoked ten. That's eleven. So you're deluding yourself, aren't you? About the amount you smoke. And a gross delusion at that, Mr Melon. Why? Why lie about it? Why say you smoke three or four when you evidently smoke – what? Fifty? Sixty? And of course he said, and then I said, did you? Or did you leave packets unsaid as a way of deceiving me? Your smoking could have something to do with the breakdown. Its effect over the years on the nervous system – and of course he said and then I said, indeed? How interesting. So the breakdown has flushed you out as a smoker. Until then you were a latent smoker. I consider that to be important progress. The next step is to get you to stop again. Then at least you'll be able to afford my fees.

Shrink 1 And I said, I've just grasped something rather interesting about your case, Mr Melon. There are one or two classic symptoms. They're of the kind we usually associate with sibling rivalry. And of course he said and I said, not in the slightest. In fact quite the contrary. Not having an actual sibling to rival meant you had to make one up. Having made him up you had to assault him for not existing. Which is precisely what you did to that famous television friend of yours who was *not* having an affair with your wife. His not having an affair was the treachery of the brother who didn't exist. If he had existed he would have affirmed the rivalry and thus his siblingness by actually having an affair with your wife and would have eventually required psychiatric help himself. As it is you've had to come in his place. In other words, you are your non-existent brother.

Shrink 2 Non-existent brother.

Shrink 1 See how it all fits together, Mr Melon.

Shrink 2 And I said, you're feeling better, and of course he said and I said, well, look at you, man. For one thing, we've stopped you smoking. I've never seen anyone not smoke as much as you're not smoking – you must be up to the two-hundred, three-hundred-a-day mark, Mark. Well done, Melon.

Shrink 1 And I said, you really must start trying to pull yourself together. Anyway, I suppose we'd better try you out on some new drugs. If those don't work we'll try some newer drugs. By the time we've discovered what effect they have on you, there'll be even newer drugs, and of course he said . . .

Shrink 2 And I said, now we start reducing the dosage of whatever it is you're on at the moment. Don't worry. We'll give you others to counter the effect of taking you off them. We might even try the same ones. That often works. The truth is, Mr Melon – the truth is you're a nuisance. And a bore. And of course he said, and I said – there. You've turned the corner. You've started to bore yourself.

Shrink 1 Bore yourself.

Shrink 2 Haven't you? A sure sign of returning health. I don't know who will be given credit for your recovery.

Shrink 1 You've been treated to a great variety of treatments.

Shrink 2 Many of them completely contradictory. One day we may know more about what we did to cure you.

Shrink 1 And then perhaps we shall discover more about what made you ill.

Shrink 2 But for the moment –

Shrink 1 All we can do –

Shrink 2 Is to congratulate ourselves. But don't you congratulate yourself, Mr Melon.

Shrink 1 We've seen enough of cases like yours to know that even when you're cured, you're not actually well.

Shrink 2 In fact you'll never be actually well again.

Shrink 1 But then you don't deserve to be, do you? After all the trouble you've given everyone.

Shrink 2 I'm sure you understand that, Mr Lemon.

Shrink 1 You're an educated man.

Shrink 2 Now go on your way, my son, and sin no more.

Shrink 1 You heard me. On your bike, and no more fucking about.

Shrink 2 You've got bills to pay, before you sleep.

Shrink 1 Bills to pay before you sleep.

Shrinks exit from where they entered.

Melon And so forth, and so forth, and so forth.
You see, ladies, how it was done! It may seem arbitrary, un-thought-out, a hop from one brutality to the other, to the mere layman, the yous and mes who never think of the need for experts in matters of this kind until we have a need for them – but – but – whatever your doubts, ladies, look at me, by God, look at me! Oh, I know what you're thinking! Why didn't someone just take the beggar by the scruff of the neck, shake him about a bit, paddle his bottom, tell him to pull his socks up, say your prayers, gentle Jesus meek and mild, look upon your little child, pity him his simply sitting, teach him, Lord, to come to Thee and so forth. Forth. Forth and forth.

Kate enters to sit on chair right.

Kate It's time to come home.

Melon Is it, love? Oh good.

Kate Come along, then.

Melon Right. But – but what about us, love? Are we going to be all right?

Kate We're going to do our best. Aren't we?

Melon But what frightens me, love, is – whether you'll be able to forgive me. That's the question. That's what's been frightening me, love. Whether you'll be able to forgive me.

Kate You were ill. So what is there to forgive?

Melon reaches out his hand to Kate. She moves to take it but before their hands join, Josh enters from right.

Melon Ah, Josh. That looks good, what is it?

Josh Well, um, cottage cheese. It's got carrots in it. And raisins.

Melon Well, I hope it tastes even more delicious than it sounds, eh?

Josh I'm glad you're back, Dad.

Melon Thank you.

Josh I'd better tell you now. I probably won't be going to university. I didn't do too well in my A levels, you see.

Melon A levels? Oh, who cares. Look at me. Ten O levels, five A levels, first-class honours degree from Cambridge, and what did it lead to? Electric shocks in a mental institution, that's what it led to. No, all I want from you, Josh, all your mother and I want from you is that you should be – be – you know. Be. Old chap.

Melon moves to embrace Josh – but before he can, something stops him and he walks away to sit on chair left. When Melon is seated, Michael enters from left.

Michael Mark. I had some idea you weren't coming in till Monday. At the top of the week.

Melon Really? Is that what we –? Well, can't do any harm to put the toe in the water, test the temperature. Can it?

Michael Still it would have given us a chance to get your office ready for you.

Melon Oh, well, it looks – it really looks –

Michael I mean your new office.

Melon Oh. Oh I – yes. I should have thought. That we might be exchanging offices –

Michael Well, not so much exchanging. Edward's in my office. You'll be in Edward's attic – as he and I both need more space. If I'm going to continue as general managing editor. And Edward's going to continue as fiction and poetry editor. When he retires – again – we'll reconsider the situation, of course. So I'm in . . .

Melon Oh, of course. And – until then – what will I be doing, Michael?

Michael What Edward was doing. Sorting out his memoirs. We both feel there's a very valuable book there, and that you're just the chap to find it. As Edward doesn't have the time at the moment. I don't quite know what else there is for you here, at Haylife and Gladstone, Mark. At the moment.

Melon No, no. That's fine. Just to be in the building and to be doing something connected with the great tradition. Helping keep it alive, it'll be a privilege, Michael, to work on Edward's memoirs, etc., etc. How's little Rufus? Marcus, Marcus. Sorry.

Michael We've found him a very good all-the-year-round boarding school. In Canada. We gather that he's showing signs of settling down.

Samantha enters from right and stops at centre when she sees Melon.

Samantha Oh. Oh, sorry. I didn't know . . .

Michael That's all right, love, I didn't either. Say hello.

Samantha Hello, Mr Melon.

Melon Hello, Sammy. Um – how's the – Shakespeare going, Sammy?

Samantha Um, well . . .

Michael Sammy and I had a little talk. She's decided to stay here and make a career in publishing.

Melon Quite right, quite right, as you've always liked books, after all –

Samantha Well, they're better than other forms of self-abuse, I suppose, Mr Melon.

Melon What?

Michael Quoting *Macbeth,* weren't you? 'This strange and self-abuse.' But the thing is we've got rather a lot to do – and I've got an author coming in any minute.

Melon Oh. Oh yes. Of course, Michael. Then I'll just –

Gladstone enters.

Gladstone Michael, Michael, she's terribly late. I've been waiting on the pavement. I do hope that lunatic Melon hasn't been in touch with . . .

Michael points out Melon to Gladstone, who then backs away.

Melon It's only me, Edward!

Michael That's all right, Edward. Mark's much better now. And we must all be kind to him. As we agreed.

Gladys (*entering*) Hello, darlings! Sorry I'm late.

Michael And how's our favourite author?

Gladstone Ah, Gladys, my dear. We were just celebrating the arrival of *The Chastity Belt*.

Michael A great title, great title for a follow-up. Sammy adored it. Didn't you, Sammy?

Samantha I thought it was the most . . .

Kate Darling, I'd rather you didn't.

Josh But Mum, I'll be back before midnight, I swear.

The alarm goes off and Melon stops it.

Melon Well, there we are, ladies. We seem to have got to the end, haven't we? May I thank you for inviting me to share my – my experiences with you. I feel oddly better for the occasion and hope that you are – none of you – any the worse for it. After all, what has happened when it comes to it? Nothing so terrible, really. Nothing so very terrible when you think about it. I mean, there I was going about my life – my happy, happy life – and then one day the earth opened at my feet and I hurtled into the – the – But on the other hand here I am back again. And where's the damage, eh, ladies? Just because I don't understand, you don't understand, and they don't understand, none of us understands why the earth opened doesn't make it any sort of disaster, or mystery even. And there is, as lots of people always say, a funny side, isn't there, ladies? I mean – well, for instance, if what had happened to me hadn't happened to me I would still be married to my Kate. And she would never, would she, have left me for Rupert, would she? It was all their worry, all their intimate conversations about me and my behaviour that brought them together. So there's a – well, if it isn't funny it's a bit of an irony at least, isn't it?

I often think about that. That's one of the things I often
think about. Perhaps that's what was intended all the
time. That she and he, he and she – and I was just their
instrument. Or God's, of course. Because we all know
God moves in a mysterious way. Especially as she, my
Kate, is going to have another baby at last. Perhaps
that's why I had to take a little punishment, so that a
new life could be brought into the world – I mean, that's
one way of looking at it, isn't it? On the other hand, it's
also possible that they really had been having an affair
all the time. Just as I suspected. Little pieces of evidence
seem to pop up now and then. But naturally I ignore
them. After all, who am I to say? Who am I to know?
The important thing is, that though she's happy at last –
deservedly happy – she's never really gone from me.
In here (*tapping his head*) or here (*touching his heart*)
I can still feel her sometimes. And I try to make the
best of things, the best of things as they really are. As I
understand them. Oh, one last thing. I've nearly finished
Edward's memoirs, which are to be published by Haylife
and Gladstone – sometime in the – we hope – in the
autumn. So you see my life goes on. And ladies, on that,
I trust, upward-beating note I take my – oh, good heavens.
I'd nearly forgotten. Your delightful Mrs Macdonald
would never have forgiven me – except I suspect that she
forgives everyone everything. Here we are – (*Takes paper
out of his pocket; reads.*) 'Next week's talk in the series
"Why me?" will be given by Mr Maxwell Dodsworth,
general manager of Floy's Brewery. The title he has
chosen is: 'One Morning I Bent to Pick a Tulip'. In it
he'll describe how the resultant back injury and his
anxiety to return to work as quickly as possible led him to
undergo a miracle cure that caused hallucination, blindness,
incontinence, obesity and finally carried him to the
very brink of death.' Obviously another story with a
comparatively happy outcome, eh, ladies? Otherwise he

wouldn't be able to come here and tell it to you, would he? And I must say, it sounds so tempting that I might well find myself back in Chichester – Cheltenham – next week. Especially if in the interim I let my tummy's memory stray to your sandwiches and cakes. Thank you for them again. And for your kind attention. Thank you, ladies and ladies, Mrs Macdonald.

Curtain.